CREATIVE PROGRAMS FOR

Life-Changing
CAMPS AND
Retreats

Student Impact Resources from Zondervan

Impact Sports

Life-Changing Camps and Retreats

Programming with Purpose

Small Group Resources, vol. 1: Walking with Christ

Small Group Resources, vol. 2: Compassion for Lost People

Small Group Resources, vol. 3: Learning to Serve

Small Group Resources, vol. 4: A Lifelong Calling

Student Ministry for the 21st Century

STUDENT IMPACT

CREATIVE PROGRAMS FOR

Life-Changing

CAMPS AND

Retreats

EVERYTHING

YOU NEED

TO LEAD

- **TWO WEEKEND RETREATS**

- **A FOUR-DAY CAMP**

- **A WEEK-LONG CAMP**

THE STUDENT IMPACT TEAM

ZondervanPublishingHouse
Grand Rapids, Michigan

A Division of HarperCollinsPublishers

WILLOW CREEK

RESOURCES

Life-Changing Camps and Retreats
Copyright © 1998 by the Willow Creek Association

Requests for information should be addressed to:
ZondervanPublishingHouse
Grand Rapids, Michigan 49530

ISBN: 0-310-20123-3

Interior design by Jack Rogers

Printed in the United States of America

98 99 00 01 02 03 04 05 /❖ML/ 10 9 8 7 6 5 4 3

To all of you who have ever served at camp and:
lost countless hours of sleep;
been the subject of a prank;
eaten too many pizzas, Oreos, and Doritos;
changed the church van's flat tire on the way to camp;
rushed an injured camper to a local emergency room;
given financially so that a student could attend camp;
cooked vats of oatmeal and washed sticky dish after sticky dish;
disciplined a rowdy student;
and sacrificed limited vacation time.

Your willingness to minister to students and model Christlikeness makes a difference. We thank God for you and cheer you on!

"Therefore, my dear brothers, stand firm. Let nothing move you. Always give yourselves fully to the work of the Lord, because you know that your labor in the Lord is not in vain."
(1 Cor. 15:58)

Table of Contents

Acknowledgments

Hundreds of people have invested their time, spiritual gifts, and energy over the years serving at numerous Student Impact camps and retreats. From administering registration to leading small groups to playing in the band to cooking meals, these unsung heroes have impacted many students' lives. The parents' team, programming and production teams, small group leaders, worship team and band members, competition directors, administrative team, and message givers play vital roles in making camp happen. If I could list all the names of the gifted men and women who have served so faithfully over the years, these pages would be full. I am so grateful for each one of you and thank you for your willingness to serve.

Troy and Tricia Murphy and Kim Anderson were the point leaders for this project. Their love for camp is obvious and I hope you sense that as you read this book. We put this material together in hopes that it would help others plan life-changing camps.

Troy's limitless creativity and leadership is evident throughout this book. Through programming, he is able to paint clear images of God for students to see and understand.

Making God's Word come alive through small groups is a special gift God has given Tricia. Most of the small group material was specially written by her to connect with the messages. I'm thankful for her servant's spirit and the valuable role she played in our ministry.

Kim organized, wrote, and edited most of the material in this book. She assisted writing *Programming with Purpose* and helped me write *Student Ministry for the 21st Century*. I'm thankful that her passion for high school students and her gift of writing is being used to provide resources for hundreds of youth workers around the country. Without Kim, these projects would not have been possible.

For the camps in this book, I am especially grateful to those who contributed in special ways:

- Dan Webster and Harvey Carey, two gifted teachers. Thanks for sharing your messages in this book.

- Jeff and Erin Frazier, Jeannie and Jarett Stevens, Diane Elliot, and Lynette Rubin for their writing contributions. It was fun having you be part of this project.

- Dave Cooke for his superb work with video and creative input over many years. God has used your gifts to help change lives.

- Bruce and Kristin Smith for their immense contributions before, during, and after most of the camps in this book.

- The prayer warriors who prayed for camp and at camp and covered our ministry in prayer.

- The men and women who generously gave financing and provided scholarships for students to attend camp.

- The programming and production team members who brainstormed and developed creative programs that drew students closer to Christ.

Planning and doing a camp is a real team effort. To the Student Impact staff and leadership team, I thank you for helping to organize, plan, pray for, and lead camps that have assisted students in becoming fully devoted followers of Christ.

Thanks again to the Zondervan team, especially Dave Lambert and Rachel Boers, for completing another great project. I'm thankful to the Willow Creek Association, particularly Doug Yonamine and Tammy Burke, for all your support and encouragement.

May this book to which so many have contributed be a tool to encourage and assist you in giving your best to whatever God has called you to do.

Serving together,

Bo Boshers
Executive Director, Student Impact
July 1997

Introduction

Great things can take place in the lives of students while they're at camp! With careful planning and with the power of the Holy Spirit, retreats and camps can facilitate spiritual growth in students' lives. Year after year, our Student Impact team marvels at the amazing ways God works through these events to reveal Himself and to touch the hearts and souls of students.

Students seem more receptive to spiritual truths when they are removed from the daily routine of their home and school environments. We need to realize that the stakes are high during those 48 hours, 4 days, or weeklong camps to which we take our students. We have a tremendous opportunity to witness life change as we build memories and ministry traditions with our students. Listen to the following testimonies:

☐ ○ ☐

When I was a freshman, my sister invited me to go on a weekend retreat with Student Impact. At the time, I wasn't a Christian. I knew there was a God, but I did not know that a personal relationship with Christ was available to me. I decided to go on the retreat just to have fun. I had met some of my sister's friends and I knew they were cool; there was something different about them. During the last message, the speaker talked about God's love and how He loved even me. I learned that God even knew the number of hairs on my head! The speaker read Psalm 139 and told me that God wanted a relationship with me. I sat there and thought, *Wow, that would be cool if that was true.* I walked back to my cabin and said to God, "If what I heard is true, then I want to feel that and want it to be a part of my life." My sister came into the cabin and asked me what I was thinking. She shared her testimony with me. I told her I wanted Christ in my life. She prayed with me and led me to Christ. Camp was the starting block for my Christian walk.

A couple of days before I went to camp, I got arrested for possession of marijuana. At camp, God began to break down the walls I had built toward Him. The speaker taught about the way I should live my life for Jesus. God convicted me during one of the messages and afterward, I called my mom and told her to throw out my drug paraphernalia and marijuana in my room at home. I decided to become a Christian. God changed my life big time at camp!

Life Change

☐ ○ ☐

I had been a Christian for awhile, but I was not growing in my faith. I went to camp and my life was radically changed. I learned about having compassion for my unchurched friends and of my purpose as a Christian. I felt touched by God's breath and energized as a Christian. Camp renewed my faith.

During our last night at camp, we all sat around a cross and worshiped God. One of the leaders challenged us to think about the sin in our lives and to write some of the sins down on a piece of paper. When we felt ready, we pinned our pieces of paper onto the cross to remind us that Christ has forgiven our sins. This was a defining moment in my Christian life.

Defining Moments

☐ ○ ☐

When I was a senior, I served as a small group leader at camp. There were two guys in my group who came to camp seeking God. During our first small group, we sat on a log by the lake. I challenged each of these guys spiritually by asking: "Where do you stand with God? What is holding you back from accepting Christ into your life?" Before camp ended, both of these guys made decisions to accept Christ.

The summer after my junior year, I went on an all-guys camping trip. The only way guys could go on this trip was to bring a non-Christian friend so there was a one-to-one ratio of Christians to non-Christians. We did lots of fun things, but the purpose of the weekend was to share the Gospel with our friends. On the last night, there was some great teaching and then we had a chance to talk one-on-one with our non-Christian friends. I shared my testimony with my friend and told him about Jesus Christ. The seed was planted in his heart.

Spiritual Challenges

---○---

I sat with my leader on a bench by the river, and she showed me how to do my first quiet time. I was a fairly new Christian at that time and unfamiliar with quiet times. She really pointed me in the right direction and helped me grow as a Christian.

It's amazing how much I grew in Christ at camp last month. In three days, my relationship with God got totally turned around and so much stronger. You can get lost in just looking for the cute guys at camp, but I know now that camp is for building relationships and growing in Christ.

Growth

---○---

On the bus ride to camp, one of the coolest guys on my team fell asleep. His shoes were off and I realized I had some red nail polish. My friend took the nail polish and painted his toes. No one gave him nail polish remover the whole week! This guy retaliated by taking my friend in her sleeping bag as she slept and placing her out on the volleyball court in the middle of camp. When she woke up, all the guys were standing around her. That's traumatic for a high school girl to be seen without her makeup on!

One night during dinner at camp, my team decided to make a grand entrance. Before camp, we had told the girls to bring their prom dresses and the guys, suits and ties. We all dressed up and marched in to dinner together. The rest of the students in the ministry couldn't believe what our team had done!

Fun

---○---

I loved sitting around a bonfire every night at camp with my friends. We sang fun camp songs and awesome worship choruses, and also spent time talking about significant things. I just remember how cool it was to all be together.

Last year, I had the opportunity to lead a small group for the first time at camp. My small group built such a level of trust and community; we totally shared our hearts. I learned how to lead by serving others. It was one of the most "impactful" experiences of my life.

Community

Retreats and camps encompass all these elements and more. Getting away to an environment free from everyday distractions allows students to develop and deepen their relationships and to focus on spiritual growth. But a retreat or camp is more than just a spiritual mountaintop experience. In fact, there is some danger involved in creating such a spiritually charged atmosphere at camp. Students get "fired up" about spiritual issues, but often burn out shortly after they return home. The flames of spiritual growth that begin at camp need to be fanned in students' lives as they strive to become fully devoted followers of Christ.

Follow-up is critical after camp. Accept our challenge to not only plan a dynamic camp or retreat, but to also think about what will happen to your students when they return to their home environment. How will you help your students keep growing during the year?

If you want to learn more about how to organize your ministry so that your students have opportunities to experience life change throughout the year, we suggest that you read *Student Ministry for the 21st Century* (Zondervan, 1997). This may be a valuable resource as you develop, strategize, and pray for your ministry's post-camp plan. Trust God to work in the hearts of your students while at camp and to assist you in helping them grow into fully devoted followers of Christ.

HOW TO USE THIS BOOK

Each of the camps described in this book have been used with great success by Student Impact, the high school ministry of Willow Creek Community Church in South Barrington, Illinois. With a weekly outreach program that extends to 32 campuses and hundreds of students and involvement of 600 core students in small groups, Student Impact is a dynamic, purpose-driven student ministry that focuses on effecting spiritual life change, one life at a time.

We do not claim to know all the answers, nor do we believe that we have tapped into some secret formula for running effective camps. But, by the grace of God, we have been able to put together some camps that God has used to bring about real life change in many high school students. In this book, we will share some important ministry values that are transferable and relevant to your ministry. We'll also walk you through four Student Impact camps, each of which has a unique focus in meeting specific student needs:

- **Set Sail**–a five-day camp that focuses on students' spiritual development and growth.
- **Impact University**–a four-day camp that teaches core students about your ministry philosophy and casts a vision for ministry.
- **Mission Impossible**–a weekend retreat for students to learn about their God-given mission and to experience community through small groups.
- **PWR**–a weekend retreat designed to equip students in their evangelism efforts and to challenge them to have compassion for their non-Christian friends.

In each camp, you will find a step-by-step description of each day and information on messages, small groups, programs, and competitions. You will also find a helpful checklist of materials needed to help you prepare for each camp or retreat.

To get the most out of this book, you need to understand our values, know the terms and definitions, and be ready to evaluate *your* ministry needs. We'll start with our values.

Understand Our Values

Student Impact's mission is to reach unbelieving high school students and help them become fully devoted followers of Jesus Christ. The strategy in fulfilling this mission is based on what we call full-cycle evangelism: a seven-step strategy in which a non-Christian (a seeker) becomes a fully devoted follower of Christ. Step #1 begins when a Christian student builds an integrity friendship with a non-Christian. In Step #2, the Christian student shares a verbal witness and God begins to work in the seeker's heart. He or she continues with steps 3 through 7: Step #3, attends Impact (a program for seekers); Step #4, accepts a spiritual challenge (at some point conversion takes place); Step #5, attends Insight (a program for believers; Step #6, gets connected to a D-Team (small group); Step #7, shares the ownership of the ministry. When the student realizes the amazing way God touched his or her life, he or she is excited to then start Step #1 with a non-Christian friend. Relationships and compassion for non-Christians fuel our strategy in reaching students for Christ. Our ministry is relationship-driven, not program-driven.

We believe high school students matter to God, and that He has entrusted us to care for His children and assist them on their spiritual journeys. What a tremendous responsibility and privilege we have as student ministers! We strive to use every opportunity God gives us to share His truth with each student who visits our ministry. We realize that we may only have one chance to touch a student's heart with the love of Christ. This requires that our ministry be purposeful and that we be prepared.

As you look at the retreats/camps in this book, notice that each programming element and activity is intended to help facilitate spiritual change in the lives of students. Rather than filling time slots when we plan each camp, we often ask the questions: "Why should we do this? What purpose will it serve? Does it keep us focused on our mission? Is it helping us build relationships?" Asking and answering these questions prevents us from planning activities that have no clear purpose. These questions will challenge you to stay focused on *your* ministry's mission.

Two of the vehicles we believe God uses to maximize life change are campus ministry and small groups. Student Impact's structure revolves around campus teams. A student is placed on a campus team according to the high school he or she attends. Campus ministry is powerful because Christian students are the ones rubbing shoulders with their non-Christian friends every day. They can band together and penetrate their campus with the love of Christ. Organizing by campus teams builds team unity and ministry momentum. You may want to consider organizing your students into campus teams for a retreat as well as the rest of your ministry year.

If your ministry focuses on one high school, you could create two teams by dividing the lower and upper classes. The freshmen and sophomores could band together and develop a plan to reach others their age with the love of Christ, while juniors and seniors may be ready for leadership roles as they continue to impact their campus for Christ.

We also believe God uses small groups to bring about life change in students. Small groups offer a safe place for students to experience care, acceptance, and true community, while being encouraged to become more like Christ. In a small group, students can challenge one another and hold each other accountable. Small groups provide opportunities for discipleship and should also teach students to become more compassionate toward their non-Christian friends. We believe balancing the scales of discipleship and evangelism can be done most effectively through the ministry of small groups.

A camp/retreat should reflect the values, vision, mission, and strategy of a ministry. If it does not, the camp/retreat will simply be a "weekend getaway" filled with unrelated, purposeless activities. Plan your camp according to *your* ministry's needs and values and you will begin to see life change in *your* students as they take steps to become fully devoted followers of Christ.

Know the Terms and Definitions

Some of the terms we use in Student Impact may be unfamiliar to you. Listed below are definitions of some of the terms you will find within each camp.

Competition

Competition in a camp setting can be a very effective team-building tool. When students are grouped according to the high school they attend, bonding takes place and tremendous team spirit is usually generated. Relationships are built through competition as students work together to ensure a team victory. Student Impact has found that students enjoy being part

of a team and want to be participants rather than spectators. Another benefit of competition is that it burns off students' energy, preparing them to be more attentive for messages and small group times.

We have listed suggested ideas for competitions at each camp, but only you can determine whether they will work for your group, location, facilities, weather, and equipment. Choose competitions that are appropriate for guys and girls to play together. For additional competition ideas, see *Impact Sports: Creative Competitions for Team Building* (Zondervan, 1997).

Concert of Prayer

A concert of prayer is a time of worship, prayer, and unity where students and leaders celebrate our great God and remember Him through the sacrament of communion. Students love to participate in a concert of prayer, especially with friends from their small groups. A concert of prayer creates an environment of special moments in which God touches hearts in unique ways.

On the last evening of each camp, Student Impact usually schedules a concert of prayer. During this time, students sit with their small groups and are led in worship with both energetic and more reflective kinds of praise choruses. They are encouraged to pray silently or with their small group members for various issues communicated from the worship leader. A concert of prayer is also a time for confession of sin, privately and within small groups, as well as a chance to make a commitment to God and the student ministry. You will need to determine the appropriate manner for your group to participate in communion according to your church or organization's policies.

Cue Sheets

A cue sheet breaks down a program into specific time slots and categories. Time slots give you an idea of approximately how many minutes it takes to complete a particular part of the program. Categories allow you to see which elements, such as videos or music, are being used in a program. Using a cue sheet helps your program sessions to stay organized and on schedule.

Cue sheets also insure that every minute is accounted for and not wasted in each program session. Every program element listed on a cue sheet should be evaluated to make sure it helps to accomplish the program's purpose. We believe your programs can become more effective in communicating God's truth by using cue sheets. We have included sample cue sheets for each program session in all four camps to assist you.

D-Teams (Small Groups)

At Student Impact, we call our small groups "D-Teams." The "D" stands for *delta*, which is Greek for "change." Each D-Team is led by an adult leader or senior student and includes two to eight students. When groups contain more than eight students, it's difficult for each student's voice to be heard.

The Bible-based curriculum included in each camp was written by Student Impact so that our D-Team sessions would closely relate to the messages in each camp. Most of the D-Team sessions in each camp follow the message times to give students the opportunity to: (1) process with their peers what they have just learned; (2) ask any questions they may have; (3) dig deeper into God's Word; and (4) hold each other accountable in taking steps of growth. D-Team leaders need to receive the D-Team material prior to camp so that they can study and prepare.

It would be best to organize small groups before arriving at camp since you'll have many other details to take care of at camp. In many cases, small groups will form naturally based on affinity and the high schools students attend. For example, freshmen like to hang out with freshmen and athletes relate to other athletes. If you are unable to organize student small groups prior to your camp, perhaps camp can be the starting place for your small group ministry. Allow your students to form their own groups and provide assistance as needed. Place a leader with each small group and try to keep the ratio five students for every leader. Be prepared to assist any students who are new or unable to find a small group.

Leaders' Meeting

Prior to camp, it is important to gather all the camp leaders for a training and informational meeting. Take the time to walk them through the entire camp schedule to help them feel informed. At this meeting, give your leaders their D-Team material as well as information on the messages, and explain their part of the Concert of Prayer. Also distribute copies of the Leaders' Responsibility Sheets (See Appendix A on page 178), which explains expectations and roles for

leaders. It is critical that the ministry director cast a vision for and clearly communicate the camp/retreat goals. Answer any questions and have leaders pray together for the upcoming camp.

At some point during each day of our camp/retreat, Student Impact holds a meeting with all the leaders. The purpose of these meetings is to keep everyone informed of the day's events and to spend some time in prayer. It is also a great time to share stories of how God is working in the lives of students and to take time to celebrate.

Messages and Rationales

At Student Impact, we believe God's Word needs to be taught with boldness. Students need to hear that God's Word is practical and relevant to their daily lives.

In each camp, we have suggested a detailed outline and biblically based text for every message. The messages relate to the camp's theme and are topical in nature. We try to limit messages to 30 minutes. You will also find rationale statements, which include the objective and main points for each message. In Student Impact, we state our rationale to the students during the message introduction so that they know where we are headed.

We encourage you to develop a rationale statement for every message given in your ministry. Doing this will keep you focused on your mission and why you are teaching what you are teaching. If you are using a guest speaker at your camp, be sure you know what he or she intends to teach. Never assume! Using a rationale statement can really help and protect you in this situation.

One-on-Ones

A one-on-one is a 15- to 30-minute conversation between a student and another student or between a student and a leader. This intentional time "forces" students to talk about significant things, not just sports or the weather. Student Impact schedules one-on-ones either after lunch or dinner during each day of camp. Our students love this time and for some, it is memorable and life-changing. Encourage your students to have one-on-ones with students or leaders whom they don't know very well. This is a great time for students who may not know many others to make new friends. It's also a great time for leaders to invest some individual time in a student. We have included a list of suggested questions for you to use during your camp's one-on-ones (See Appendix B on page 180).

Team Time
During each camp, Student Impact encourages campus teams to meet together for four reasons: (1) to build team unity; (2) to get to know one another better; (3) to pray for their campus; and (4) to have fun together. Team time is led by the campus director (one who leads a campus team) and may involve vision-casting, prayer, introduction of new team members, announcements, further teaching related to the camp theme, and team goals for post-camp sessions. Team time after camp can keep building momentum in your ministry and encourage friendships to continue developing.

Worship
In a purpose-driven student ministry, students learn how to truly worship the Lord and are Spirit-led by the worship leader to focus on Him. In every program in each of the camps, we encourage you to lead your students in meaningful worship. We realize that music styles vary from ministry to ministry and often change. For this reason, we do not give you specific worship orders in each program, but have provided a suggested chorus list (See Appendix C on page 181) that will help you plan your worship segments.
We value the role worship plays in drawing students closer to Christ. We hope that you, too, will desire to lead worship in a way that assists your students in becoming fully devoted followers of Him.

Evaluate *Your* Ministry Needs
God's unique fingerprint is on each student ministry. Your students, leaders, church, location, and ministry philosophy are unlike any other student ministry in the world. Take some time to quiet yourself before the Lord to discern the particular vision, mission, and strategy He has entrusted to your ministry. This book will be ineffective if you simply "cookie cutter" the camps included. These camps will help you take the next steps in your ministry. When you recognize *your* ministry's purpose, you can take the ideas and outlines of these four Student Impact camps and ask God to lead you as you plan your own camp.
You probably will think of more creative

ideas or a better way to do certain elements than what we have listed. Our prayers are that this book will stir and challenge you to figure out how to make the ideas found here come alive for the students in your ministry.

Remember, the stakes are high, so keep the bar of excellence raised in all you do. We join you and cheer you on in your efforts to make a difference in the lives of high school students.

Managing a Retreat/Camp

The highlight for me at our retreat was the Saturday night Concert of Prayer. To see hundreds of high school students, arms around each other, singing to the Lord with all their hearts, was an awesome experience. To me, that is what student ministry is all about.

One of my favorite moments at camp was seeing eleven buses, loaded with tired, but spiritually energized, students, pulling out of the camp parking lot heading for home. I knew at that moment that God had done amazing things in each of their lives and that they would never be the same again.

Moments like these generally don't just "happen." At Student Impact, we strategically plan for, pray for, create, build, and design the right environments for moments to occur. We believe that every youth worker can organize an effective and purposeful retreat if he or she takes five very important steps: define the purpose; prepare in advance; program for success; promote the event; and pray.

Define the Purpose

The first step in planning a purpose-driven retreat is to ask yourself some important questions which will help you to define the retreat's purpose and general makeup.

The following questions will get you thinking about ways to develop a purpose-driven retreat and assist you in being intentional at camp:

1. What do you want to accomplish with this retreat/camp?
2. What do you want the students to walk away with?
3. What are your ministry goals in relationship to this retreat/camp?
4. How many students do you think will attend?
5. How many leaders are available?
6. What would be a good, contemporary theme that will connect with students?
7. How can you make your theme come alive?
8. What is the best environment to accomplish your overall goals?
9. What resources do you have to contribute to this retreat/camp?
   - Monetary?
   - Talent? (Musicians, speakers, comedians, announcers, actors)
   - Volunteers?
   - Facility?
   - Time?
10. Who is the camp target–believers, seekers, or both? Where are your students at spiritually? What are their needs?
11. What is your ministry's vision, mission, and strategy? How does camp fit into it?
12. How do you define "success" at camp?

After you determine the "why" and "what" of a retreat by asking these kinds of tough questions, you can then pick a theme based on the retreat's purpose. Creating a theme helps the programming team to plan more creative and effective programs.

Evaluate your geographical location and use it to your benefit whenever possible. For example, if your ministry is near an ocean, try using some sort of beach theme. You need to create a theme for camp that will excite students and relate to their culture. Student Impact used an Olympic theme to coincide with the summer Olympics and built this theme around being a champion for Christ.

In spite of the fun we have had with different themes over the years, there has always been a biblical principle woven carefully into the fabric of each camp/retreat. Camp themes should have a deeper spiritual meaning and tie into your ministry's purpose.

Prepare in Advance

After defining the purpose and picking a theme, the next important and often overlooked step is to prepare in advance. There are no shortcuts for the planning stage of building a successful camp or retreat. It is the detailed work at this stage that sets apart the novice from the professional.

Before we look into the specifics of preparation, there is a retreat option that might be more in line with your needs. You may want to consider hiring a professional meeting planner who will assist you in your overall retreat management, including site selection, contract negotiation, registration, and on-site administration. A meeting planner is especially helpful if you use a hotel facility. Generally, hotels demand a higher level of management and details, which a meeting planner is prepared to coordinate. In addition, a meeting planner may be able to negotiate a better contract with a hotel. Incidentally, his or her fee varies based on the amount of responsibility that you delegate to him or her.

One of the most practical and helpful tools for effective retreat planning is a Retreat/Camp Notebook. Fill it with the following general categories: timeline, budget, facility, transportation, housing, food, meeting space, contracts, printed materials, and registration.

Timeline
As you plan a retreat with your youth ministry team, first develop a timeline (see Appendix D on page 182). All you need to do is plug in the dates when each of these tasks need to be completed. Your schedule will vary depending on your group size and specifics of the camp/ retreat. Keep in mind that it is never too early to plan ahead. It is easier to make arrangements and alter them slightly than to be scrambling wildly to pull something together at the last minute.

Budget
Although accurate budgets are sometimes difficult to estimate and time-consuming to develop, they are essential to a financially successful camp/retreat. A basic formula that Student Impact uses is this: All expenses divided by the lowest number of students who might attend the retreat. That way, if you only meet your minimum student attendance, you will still make your budget. Your financial camp goal should be to at least cover costs and break even. Before sitting down to develop a budget, you need to address some basic issues:

1. What is a reasonable amount to charge the students for the retreat?
2. Do you want to charge your leaders to attend the event? If so, how much?
3. Do you have any scholarships or money set aside for student assistance? If so, how much?
4. Based upon the answers to the previous questions and given the size of your group, what type of facility would be the most appropriate: tents, rustic camp, retreat center, hotel? The next step is to contact some of the facilities and get a general price for room, board, and meeting space. (Be aware that with hotels, it is sometimes less expensive to

eat more. As your food dollars go up, your meeting space charges go down.)
5. Use a Retreat Budget Worksheet (See Appendix E on page 183) as a basis for your budget and determine your cost and your break-even price. Then, just to be on the safe side and to account for any unexpected costs, round up to a comfortable number.

Facility
Your facility is your home away from home, so it needs to be comfortable for you as well as your students. If you are uncomfortable because it is 20 degrees below zero and you are staying in a drafty barn with no heat, you probably won't have much opportunity to impact students' lives. Conversely, if you are staying at the Hilton and are worried about students breaking the chandeliers as they swing from the ceiling, you most likely will have a nervous breakdown and drive yourself crazy. In other words, it is important to use good judgment on appropriate sites for your camp or retreat.

Once Student Impact narrows down the meeting facilities, our planning team does a site inspection to make sure that it will meet our needs. Then, as we are going through the sleeping rooms, general session room, and meeting space, we envision what it will be like with 500+ students. Is there enough space in the halls? Are we staying too close to other guests? If the worst damage does occur, what will it cost us? With those answers in mind, we determine if the site is the right place for us. Then, we negotiate the per-person price. While camps and retreat facilities often have a semi-set fee including housing and all meals, everything at hotels is generally a la carte.

The rule of thumb on negotiation is to keep working the formulas and numbers until you and the site manager are happy. You want to walk away knowing that you received a fair deal and that your needs will be met. One other helpful hint: Though hotels are generally more work on the front-end, a reputable hotel lives to serve its clients and will bend over backward to do so. By the same token, retreat and camping facilities vary greatly. Investigate the management and get to know the person who will be facilitating your group. Try to build a long-term relationship with a facility and its staff.

Transportation
Depending on the size of your group and the distance of your travel, transportation needs can

vary greatly. You may want to recruit parents and leaders to drive your students to the retreat. Or, a school bus might be fun. If you are going a distance and have 47 people (and their baggage) you might consider calling a large transportation company such as Greyhound. When Student Impact priced transportation needs for our last retreat, we found that the Greyhound price was considerably less than school buses, and we didn't have to rent separate vehicles for luggage. If your group is large, consider color-coding luggage according to campus teams. On each piece of luggage, place a colored piece of yarn according to the luggage owner's campus team.

As with the facility, organizing your transportation needs well in advance will save you many hours of undue stress. You will also spare yourself stress if you incur the cost for reliable transportation. Parents feel more confident and relaxed knowing their children are traveling in a safe, reliable vehicle. Be wise in this area and never take safety for granted.

Housing

After the facility is selected, Student Impact leaves specific housing assignments until the last minute since we only want to do this task once. If you assign housing too early and have a few more students join, it can be a real annoyance to do it all again. We generally select locations (girls in one area, guys in another) and the number of leaders per dorm and area. Then we wait until our cutoff date to assign the rooms. We try to keep a ratio of five students to every leader as we organize housing.

Food

As mentioned before, you may have a prepackaged program with no choice on food selection. In that case, you might want to ask the site what food will be served just to make sure that you will have appropriate food for your group. Student Impact always reminds the facility that these are growing students with hearty appetites. We request that healthy food be served as much as possible (salads and fresh fruits) rather than excessive junk food.

Depending on your facility, you may or may not be able to supplement meals. Some facilities permit homemade goodies. Others only allow packaged things to sell, like candy bars. Most sites allow students to bring their own snacks.

Meeting Space

Appropriate meeting space is very important. Will you always meet as a large group or do you need break-out rooms? If so, how many and when? These are questions that the facility will want to know. If you are in a hotel, they will want your exact schedule in case another group is sharing space with you. If you are in a camp setting, you usually have more flexibility with a 24-hour reserve on your meeting space, meaning that you have it during the entire time you are on site.

The next thing that you will need to determine is your room setup. Do you need chairs, and if so, how many? A stage or platform? If so, what size? Skirted tables? If so, how many and where? Audiovisual equipment?

If you're staying in a hotel, you will probably not be charged for chairs or tables. You will want to keep a copy of the facilities' meeting space in your Retreat/Camp Notebook. This sheet shows the general footage and how many people will fit in each room with the different setup styles available: theater (all chairs facing one direction); classroom (tables and chairs); in the round (circles of chairs); round tables of eight or nine (round tables with eight or nine chairs); or cocktail rounds (round tables with three or four chairs). Then, on your final schedule you can assign rooms to groups and specify how you want each room set up. (See Appendix F on page 184 for a copy of a room layout with seating possibilities.) Always check the room setup well before a program session begins. Never assume the facility personnel will cover every detail. It would be a shame if students could not hear the message or see the stage.

Staging as well as audiovisual equipment, flip charts, screens, and sound systems (other than the "house" system) generally have a fee associated with them. To avoid the padded cost of the facility's equipment, try renting equipment locally or bringing in your own.

The most important aspect of dealing with meeting space is to keep your contact at the selected facility informed. The facility will probably need your exact schedule in advance (two weeks to one month). If you have a similar schedule from a prior event, give it to your facility contact when you are negotiating a contract to indicate what type of space you used in the past and your program requirements. Keeping the value of excellence applies to the meeting space and room setup. We define excellence as doing the best with what you have. Show students that you are prepared in this area and doing your best with the facility available.

Contracts
Keep a copy of each of your contracts in your Retreat/Camp Notebook for quick reference. You should have contracts for each of the following: the facility, speakers, musicians, and transportation. A contract serves two purposes–clarification and instructions. Map out any specifics related to services, fees, special circumstances, and benefits. Where possible, you may want to include a clause for Christian arbitration in case of a dispute. (See Appendix G on page 185 for a sample speaker contract.)

Printed Materials
It is important that your printed materials be done with excellence. Students will see the effort you put into preparing the brochures and materials. Keep a clean copy of all your brochures, memos, schedules, artwork, and curriculum in your Retreat/Camp Notebook. If you run out of one of these, you will have the black-and-white original ready to photocopy. This section of your notebook is also a great place for phone numbers, camp maps and directions, and any other miscellaneous paperwork that might be needed.

Registration
From the moment students walk in the door to register, your retreat/camp has begun. Registration should be a fun and inviting place that sets the stage for your event and shows parents that you are prepared. Parents need to feel assured as they drop their children off for the retreat that you are organized and ready to take responsibility. Be sure to provide parents with information sheets that include the facility location, phone number, and emergency information.

Try to make registration a festive and enjoyable process. Do as much preparation work ahead of time so students do not have to wait longer than necessary. First, assemble student packets, which include rooming and transportation assignments, a camp schedule, and curriculum. Second, lay out your floor plan so that all activities can be done in an orderly fashion. Third, fill each station with *trained* volunteers so that the process is efficient.

On page 186 (Appendix H), you'll find a sample Student Impact floor plan for registration. We set up a luggage holding area by gender and

the students then went to the registration tables where they paid off their camp balances, verified their parents' consent form (see Appendix I on page 187), and picked up their packets with room and transportation information. Students then proceeded to the nurse's station to register any medications that they brought to the retreat. We notify students that any unregistered medications will be confiscated. Also, the nurse should keep a cooler ready in case a student has a medication that needs to be refrigerated. The last table is the solution table. Here we have a staff person who has all the answers . . . hopefully!

Program for Success
Programming is a key tool for a life-changing camp/retreat. For a program to be successful, the elements used must help accomplish the purpose; the mission must be clear. As mentioned before, the camp/retreat begins the moment the students register and ends when their parents load them into their cars to go home. At Student Impact, we use a storyboard method of program organization.

Long before the camp/retreat, we pack a small room with creative people (who understand our mission) for a three-hour brainstorming session where we storyboard our event. This meeting is called the Program Development Meeting (PDM). Before we start filling in the storyboard, we all start on the same page with what we call the rationale; the "why" and "what" for the event. Sometimes the Program Director comes into the meeting with the rationale. Other times, the PDM team develops it on the spot. With the rationale clear in everyone's mind, the PDM team maps out the specifics of the event. The overall time frame for the camp/retreat is written on colored notecards and pinned to a wall. Then we walk through the event, coming up with ideas to make it fun and exciting for students. Each suggestion then makes its way to a card pinned on the board (usually with a point person's name on it). The general sessions are slotted, but the Cue Sheets are usually completed at a second meeting dedicated just to general sessions. Over the next couple of hours, the storyboard fills up and our program unfolds.

After PDM comes the detailed work of figuring out who is going to do what, when, and how. The PDM team lays out a timeline and lists all the equipment needed and areas of responsibility. Last of all, the PDM team lays out contingency plans for unexpected problems. With smaller groups it is a little easier to get away with last-minute changes. However, the larger the group, the more difficult it is to "flex" with emergencies. Planning alternative options can be a lifesaver.

Programming for success will look different for every group. Remember, programs need not be costly or complex. Be wise in the people you select to sing, act, or give messages. Make sure that they walk authentically with Christ. If you are using a guest speaker, ask for his or her rationale (message objective and outline) for each message and give him or her program cue sheets.

Promote the Event

The promotion of your camp/retreat should definitely communicate excitement and fun, but it should also emphasize the life change that takes place at camp. Ask students who have experienced life change at camp to share their stories in front of the group as a way to promote an upcoming camp/retreat.

When you promote the camp via video, written material, or other medium, be sure to tell students the purpose of your event and what it will include. They need to know that they are not just coming for a weekend of skiing or surfing, but to an event that will hopefully draw them closer to God. Don't be afraid of scaring away seekers; it is better that they know in advance so that they come with the right expectations.

Promotion of a camp/retreat largely depends upon the size and general makeup of your group. At Student Impact, we develop a marketing strategy at our PDM meetings and do a media "rollout" over the weeks and months prior to the event. For example, our video team used booming music and "spy-looking" staff photos to promote our Mission Impossible retreat. We shoot videos and take pictures at each camp so that we can use those images to promote the following year's camp. In addition to our videos, we have announcements at our weekly programs, handouts, registration forms, student testimonies, and signs.

Perhaps the most effective method of promoting an event, however, is the personal invitations from our staff and core students. The media blitz sets the stage, but the personal invitation gets students to cross the line. The key to getting the leaders and students to the event is to keep them informed and excited.

Another key to camp/retreat promotion is making sure students have enough time to respond. Choose your deadline with your facility's requirements in mind. Hotels require guarantees two to four weeks in advance. Retreat centers usually are more flexible and may require one week's notice. Establish your policy and then stick to it as close as possible.

Pray

Although it goes without saying, prayer is the power that drives any student ministry . . . and camp. Before leaving for a camp or retreat, Student Impact asks parents, church staff, and the congregation to pray for all our special needs. Here are a few of the areas where we ask everyone to focus their prayers.

Pray for Wisdom

From our PDM meeting forward, we pray that God will be integrated in every aspect of our program. We need wisdom to carefully and creatively design an environment where God will be glorified and His principles taught.

Pray for Safety

We never consider our students' safety to be a given. Our prayers are that God will keep our students safe from the time they come into our care to the time they open their own front door. We constantly evaluate our part in keeping our students safe and pray for God to do the rest.

Pray for Servant Attitudes

Student Impact's philosophy for event planning is to plan, plan, plan, and then, at the actual event, be flexible. We pray that all those involved in planning and leading camp will have servant attitudes and that they will be prepared to do "whatever it takes" to minister to students. When a portion of a program gets cut at the last minute, its contributors may feel frustrated or hurt, losing perspective that the decision is not a quality or value issue. We pray that God will keep us all humble and flexible in the midst of potential changes.

Pray for Life Change

We pray that God will significantly impact our students' lives as well as our own. At Student Impact, we plan, program, create, and labor to build a receptive environment for spiritual growth. However, no amount of effort on our part will touch the heart of a student; that job is left for the Holy Spirit alone.

How Do We Measure Success?

We have looked at what it takes to create, program, organize, and execute a successful retreat/camp. But, how do we measure success? There are four questions you can ask yourself in order to help measure the success of your camp/retreat:

1. Was God's Word communicated in a clear and relevant way?
2. Did your camp meet your goals and did it stay focused on your mission?
3. Were all aspects of the camp done with excellence (defined as doing the best with what you have)? Do you think God would say, "Well done"?
4. Were decisions and commitments made by students and leaders to become more devoted to Christ?

After camp, take time to evaluate all aspects of camp. What changes are needed for next year's camp? Be sure to not only evaluate but to celebrate. Every camp/retreat has its potholes along the way. It is the *totality* of the event that you must use as its measurement. If you are turning students' hearts toward God and meeting your goals and expectations, you have hit the mark and God is pleased.

Setsail

Set Sail

Camp Summary: Using a sailing theme, this camp helps students identify their spiritual condition and learn how to navigate the storms of life.

Length of Camp: Five days.

Target Audience: Christian students who want to grow in their faith and spiritually sensitive non-Christian students who have a desire to know more about God.

Facility Requirements: A cabin or retreat center. Being near water and having access to sailboats or canoes would visually enhance the camp theme.

Camp Objectives:
- To help seeking and believing students identify where they are on their spiritual journeys.
- To challenge each student to take a stand for Christ and commit to becoming a fully devoted follower of Christ.
- To build relationships and unity among students.
- To give leaders opportunities to invest in the lives of students.

Introduction

"The wind of God is always blowing . . .
but you must hoist your sail."

François Fénelon (1651–1715)

From *Draper's Book of Quotations for the Christian World* by Edythe Draper (Tyndale, 1992, p. 295).

An endless ocean spills over the horizon, spreading its waiting arms, inviting you to explore. You glance over your shoulder at the safe harbor and then back at the ocean. There's something pulling you out. You can't explain it. You make one final inspection of your instruments. You check your emergency kit. You slip on your life jacket, untie the bowline knot, and your boat slowly drifts out into the vast turquoise waters that await. You raise your sails and the wind immediately inflates them as they unfurl. Gentle waves slap the side of your boat as you inhale the refreshing ocean air. It's just you and the wind. You've set sail.

If you have experienced the exhilaration of setting sail on the open waters, you will have the advantage of bringing your own experience to this camp. In this five-day camp, you will help your students "set sail" by focusing on four spiritual conditions:

- **On the Dock**–The student is not a Christian. He or she is not even in the boat.
- **Tied to the Dock**–The Christian student is pretending or "playing the Christian game." He or she is in the boat but not doing anything to grow spiritually.
- **Dead in the Water**–The Christian student is in the boat out on the lake, but there is no wind in the sails. The boat does not seem to be going anywhere. The desire to "sail" is there, but perhaps the student feels stuck on a sandbar.
- **Sailing on Open Waters**–The Christian student is growing and developing a relationship with Jesus Christ. He or she is on the way to becoming a Fully Devoted Follower of Christ (FDF).

As you read through these next pages, you will get a clearer picture of how to coordinate the programming elements, messages, competition, and small groups. Prepare to leave shore. You're about to set sail!

 # Camp Checklist

ACTIVITIES
- __ Marshmallows, chocolate bars, and graham crackers for s'mores
- __ Movie to fit nautical theme
- __ Elements for communion

COMPETITION
- __ 50 ft. rope for tug-of-war
- __ Bandana
- __ Volleyball and volleyball net
- __ 4 ft. x 30 ft. sheet of plastic for slip n' slide
- __ Dish soap or baby oil
- __ Score cards numbered 1 to 10
- __ Canoes and paddles

D-TEAMS
- __ Posterboard for signs
- __ Set Sail map
- __ Nautical equipment
- __ Rope for bowline knot
- __ Crayons and markers
- __ Material (sheets or tagboard) for flags

EMERGENCIES
- __ First Aid Kit
- __ Names and phone numbers of each camper's parent or guardian
- __ Name and directions to nearest hospital from campsite

HANDOUTS AND SUPPLIES
- __ Student notebooks
- __ Leader Responsibility Sheets
- __ Extra Bibles
- __ Camera and/or video
- __ Copies of Student Notes #1, #2, and #3

PROGRAMS
- __ Musical instruments
- __ Nautical props for stage
- __ Sailing video
- __ Walk-in music as students enter program
- __ Song sheets or slides for worship choruses
- __ Sailing clothes/outfits for band members and host

REGISTRATION
- __ Completed permission slips from each camper and leader
- __ Room assignments
- __ Petty cash box to collect remaining payments for camp

VEHICLES
- __ Maps to campsite
- __ Insurance documents
- __ Money for gas and tolls

 This is a sample letter we gave to all D-Team leaders at a meeting prior to camp. Along with this letter leaders also received D-Team material to study and prepare.

Dear D-Team Leader:

After many weeks of prayer, preparation, and trying to get your students to turn in their registration forms, Set Sail is almost here. As you think about the upcoming camp, you probably feel a sense of anticipation as well as nervousness. Take a deep breath and relax–you don't have to lead on your own. Relying on the Holy Spirit is the most important thing you can do as you lead your students during our time at camp.

At this retreat, you will help your students determine their spiritual condition by looking at four sailing positions:

- **On the Dock**–The student is not a Christian. He or she is not even in the boat.
- **Tied to the Dock**–The Christian student is pretending or "playing the Christian game." He or she is in the boat but not doing anything to grow spiritually.
- **Dead in the Water**–The Christian student is in the boat out on the lake, but there is no wind in the sails. The boat does not seem to be going anywhere. The desire to "sail" is there, but perhaps the student feels stuck on a sandbar.
- **Sailing on the Open Waters**–The Christian student is growing and developing a relationship with Jesus Christ. He or she is on the way to becoming a Fully Devoted Follower of Christ (FDF).

Before you try to help your students identify their spiritual condition, take a look at your own spiritual condition. Where are you right now? Are you "Sailing on the Open Waters" or "Dead in the Water"? Make sure that your life is in order and that you are taking steps to grow in your faith.

When you are spiritually prepared, you can then lead others. Set aside time this week to listen to how God wants you to lead and shepherd the students He has entrusted to your care. Spend time praying for the students in your D-Team, asking God to draw them closer to Him. Also, pray that

- the students who have not yet accepted Christ will come to know Him at this retreat.
- the students who are trying out D-Teams for the first time will have a positive experience.
- the students will identify their spiritual sailing position and determine appropriate steps of growth.
- the message givers will communicate God's Word clearly and will be empowered by Him.
- there will be safety in travel.
- our ministry will receive protection.
- our leaders will have direction, discernment, and strength.

During Set Sail, you will have the privilege of leading the students in your D-Team and helping them to become fully devoted followers of Christ. Your D-Team should sit together during mealtimes, the main sessions, and at the Concert of Prayer. Because you will be together during these sessions, you will have the opportunity to be creative and "own" your meeting area by decorating it or bringing notes or small gifts to your students each session. Keep the sailing theme in mind as you plan.

The D-Team material will give you all the information and ideas you will need to lead your D-Team throughout the week. There are also leadership meetings scheduled each day to keep you informed of the day's activities and also to answer any questions you may have. The following checklist will help you remember your main responsibilities for each session:

- Be prepared spiritually. Set aside time to pray and listen to God.
- Bring something to decorate your meeting area for each session. Possible ideas: personal notes, candy, gum, toy sailboats, pictures, etc. Be creative!
- Study the D-Team curriculum before you arrive at camp. You will find suggested questions and Scriptures to use in each D-Team so familiarize yourself with the material.
- Encourage students to be on time to all sessions and to bring their notebooks and Bibles. Lead by example.

Our time together is going to be incredible! Thank you for your commitment and passion to see high school students grow into fully devoted followers of Christ. Your role is so important and we greatly value and appreciate you. It will be exciting to serve together with you and to witness the amazing ways God is going to work through you to impact students' lives! Get ready to Set Sail!

 # Camp Overview

Theme

The camp theme uses sailing terminology to illustrate how to live the Christian faith and prepare for the storms that will come our way in life. The sailing theme will really come alive if leaders and students are encouraged to dress in sailing clothing. You'll probably see a lot of Hawaiian shirts, leis, sailor hats, deck shoes, and "Gilligan's gear." Instead of cruise wear, some may opt for the pirate-at-sea look and dress like Captain Hook. It's always fun to give students and leaders the freedom to express their creativity.

Handouts

Every student should be given some kind of handout or notebook to use for taking notes or journaling. You may want to include your retreat schedule in this handout as well as camp rules, a camp map, and information on various issues. Encourage students to bring their notebooks to all sessions and D-Teams.

In Student Impact, we called our notebook a Logbook to fit with the sailing theme. Here are a few ideas for designing your Logbook:

- Develop written material and print into booklet form.
- Make stickers with the camp logo and stick them onto plain, inexpensive notebooks. Students can use this for their Logbook.
- Screen the camp logo onto 5 1/2" x 8 1/2" three-ring notebooks and build this expense into camp costs.

Take-Away

Consider giving each student some kind of tangible reminder of their camp experience. A take-away object plays an important part in reminding students of their time at camp and how God worked. Some possible ideas for a take-away for this camp include a small anchor to remind students to stay anchored in Christ; a bowline knot to signify a tight relationship with Christ; a small compass to point students toward Christ; a toy sailboat or some other sailing-related item that would be meaningful for your students.

Schedule

A sample daily schedule used by Student Impact for Set Sail is included as a guideline to help you develop your own schedule. While schedules can be restrictive at times, they will keep your leaders and students organized each day and help make your time together purposeful.

Morning Worship

Throughout the week, give your students an opportunity to meet together before breakfast for worship and prayer. While it should be optional, it is a great way for your students to begin the day and turn their focus toward God and His creation. If the weather permits, meet outside and keep the format simple. Find someone who can play an acoustic guitar and is willing to lead several familiar worship songs. Throughout the 45 minutes, allow students time to share what they have been learning and the life-changing decisions that may have been made the night before.

Competition

Brainstorm with your leadership team a competitive activity in which all your students will enjoy participating.

Student Impact kept a nautical theme in mind when naming teams: The North Pier Islanders; The East Marina Cannibals; The South Harbor Pirates; and The West Port Sailors. Remember to score points so that you can announce the winning team daily and the camp champions at the end of the week.

Because this camp may be on or near water, it may be fun to use a water theme for competition. Here are a few suggestions:

- Beach volleyball tournament (two on two; four on four; or full teams of six)
- Beachfront tug-of-war
- Swim relays and canoe races
- Slip n' Slide Contest
- Bellyflop and Diving Contest

D-Teams

Throughout the week, D-Teams (small groups) give students a chance to discuss and apply what they are learning. The following descriptions give an overview of the D-Teams for the week:

D-Team #1–Know the Crew
During this D-Team, your leaders will get to know any new students and also discuss each student's expectations for the week.

D-Team #2–Set Sail Walk
During this D-Team, there will be four stations for your students to learn about and then determine where they are "docked" as well as where they are sailing with their lives.

This D-Team requires special preparation. You will need to make a sign to put at each station as described on page 36. The distance these stations should be placed apart from each other is based on the number of students who will be at each station. You will want students to be able to talk without disturbing another D-Team. If the D-Team experience is scheduled for the evening, you will need to illuminate the signs so students can read them.

You will also need to draw a map of your campsite depicting the four stations which describe spiritual conditions or use the one on page 37. Make a copy for each D-Team.

D-Team #3–Sailing Clothing
During this D-Team, students will focus on what kinds of clothes they need to wear for sailing and then relate the clothing to the importance of putting on the armor of God.

D-Team #4–Islands of Safety
During this D-Team, students will focus on the islands that serve as havens for us in the storms of life.

D-Team #5–First Things First
During this D-Team, you will stress the importance of prioritizing our lives.

D-Team #6–Bowline Knot
During this D-Team, you will discuss the need to have a tight relationship with Jesus Christ.

D-Team #7–Signal Flags
During this D-Team, you will give your students the opportunity to design a flag that represents who they are and their relationship with Jesus Christ.

Programs

All programming elements are designed to move each student emotionally and intellectually to see God's love by exposing God's truth in a relevant, practical way through the communicative arts. Each program points students toward a basic biblical truth. Sample Cue Sheets include suggested program orders.

Here are a few ideas, materials, and

props you may want to use in planning your programs:

Ideas

1. To generate ideas for the programs, the Student Impact staff team located an accomplished sailor and spent some time with him on his sailboat. It was a great team builder activity, and he taught us some basics about sailing, like how to tie a bowline knot, how to read the wind, and what sailing clothing and equipment we needed. We even interviewed him and used the interview to promote the camp.
2. If you do not know a sailor, check out some books on sailing from your local library and familiarize yourself and your programming team with sailing terms.
3. Rent sailing "how-to" videos from your local video store and any sailing related movies, such as *White Squall*, *What About Bob*, *Captain Ron*, or *Captain Hook* to gather information on sailing.
4. Watch "Gilligan's Island" and "The Love Boat" reruns to get ideas on island and cruise living.

Materials/ Props

Try to develop the nautical theme visually. Identify any sailing equipment and related items you can use to decorate the stage. We used fishnets and a large captain's wheel onstage. We also fired a cannon (like a pirate's ship) at the start of each program. Other possible prop ideas include: oars, buoys, life jackets, anchors, compasses, foghorns, canoes, or sails.

Messages

Four morning messages and four evening messages are included in this camp. Try to make all of your teaching times interactive and creative. Use the material provided, but take time to hear what the Holy Spirit wants to communicate to your students through you. Encourage your students to take notes in their Logbooks.

The morning messages are designed to be given by four leaders and should last for a maximum of 30 minutes. Each leader will be responsible for delivering the same message every morning to a different group of students. Choose four locations for students to rotate through for each of the four morning sessions. This style gives your students a variety of settings and allows your leaders to work on and improve their message deliveries. Each morning message focuses on a different biblical legend who has weathered various storms. These are called "Riders of the Storm."

The evening messages are designed to include all your students. Keep in mind that at the end of the day your students will be either really tired or really wired. Be sure to gauge the energy level each night. Keep evening messages to 30 minutes in length. In the evening, students will learn how to set sail and navigate the storms of their lives.

Here are brief summaries of the evening and morning messages:

Evening Message #1–Setting Sail
Students will identify their spiritual condition as they examine four possible sailing positions in this message.

Morning Message #1–Rider of the Storm: Moses
Storms can be very challenging for us, but they can be even harder to weather when the world is telling us how to respond. In this message, you will give your students an encouraging look at the life of Moses, who stepped down from royalty and life security to follow God's call for his life.

Evening Message #2–Storms of Life
In this message, you will offer your students some hope and a few practical tools to weather the storms of life.

Morning Message #2–Rider of the Storm: Gideon

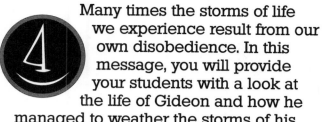 Many times the storms of life we experience result from our own disobedience. In this message, you will provide your students with a look at the life of Gideon and how he managed to weather the storms of his life.

Evening Message #3–Priorities: First Things First
By adopting two important principles, students will learn how to live well-ordered lives.

Morning Message #3–Rider of the Storm: Noah
Sometimes during the storms of life, we feel alone. In this message, you will encourage your students by telling them the story of how God called Noah alone for a specific purpose.

Evening Message #4–Nail Your Colors
In this message, you will share how your students can begin or continue to set sail in their spiritual lives by making one important commitment.

Morning Message #4–Rider of the Storm: Abraham
In this message, you will teach students about Abraham, another "Rider of the Storm," and why he was known as a man of faith.

Evening Activities
For each day, we list a suggested evening activity. Plan to do a cabin check every night and make sure that each student is in his or her cabin. You can expect high school students to pull pranks like cabin raids even after "lights out." Think about how you and your team will handle these kinds of issues before the camp begins.

Day One

Schedule

7:00 AM	Registration
8:00 AM	Buses Leave
Noon	Lunch Stop
1:00 PM	Reload Buses
3:00 PM	Arrive at Camp
3:15 PM	Opening Ceremonies
4:00 PM	Team Time
5:30 PM	Dinner
6:30 PM	Cabin Check-In

7:30 PM	D-Team #1– **Know the Crew**
9:00 PM	Evening Session– **Setting Sail**
10:30 PM	D-Team #2– **Set Sail Walk**
11:30 PM	Bonfire
12:00 AM	Cabin Check
1:00 AM	Lights Out

Day One
Opening Ceremonies

Program Cue Sheet

TIME	PROGRAM ELEMENT
3:15 PM	**DOORS OPEN/WALK-IN** Select some "high-energy" Christian music.
3:25 PM	**VIDEO** Show a sailing video. Check your local video store to see what kind of sailing footage might be available.
3:30 PM	**WELCOME** Host welcomes the students to camp and introduces the teams (with new nautical names for camp). Encourage leaders to dress according to their team's theme to generate spirit. Bring the leaders up front and introduce them.
3:50 PM	**RULES AND CAMP SCHEDULE** Host explains camp rules and expectations including the three Ms: 1. Be at all **m**eals. 2. Be at all **m**eetings. 3. Be **m**odest in all you do and say.
4:00 PM	**PRAY AND DISMISS** Host prays and gives the schedule for the rest of the day. As students leave, give them their Logbooks for the week.

Team Time

Use this time for campus teams to meet separately. Introduce any new students and leaders. Team leaders should take care of any administrative details, like lost luggage or lodging problems. Determine a location for D-Team meetings as well as any team rules. Allow your students to ask questions.

Day One
D-Team # 1–Know the Crew

Objective
During this first D-Team, you and your students will get to know any new people who have joined your student ministry for the first time. You will also ask students to share their expectations for the week. Don't be discouraged if your students' expectations aren't focused on spiritual growth–you've got the next five days to influence their hearts!

Materials Needed
No materials needed.

Get to Know Your Crew Members
Take 10-15 minutes to have your students introduce themselves and share one thing they know about sailing. Then ask each student what his or her expectations are for the next five days. Record each of these for review later to see if you can help meet those expectations during the camp.

In Closing
Close in prayer, asking God to do irreversible things in your students' lives these next few days.

Day One
Evening Session # 1

Program Cue Sheet

TIME	PROGRAM ELEMENT
7:45 PM	**LEADERS' MEETING** Student Minister
8:45 PM	**DOORS OPEN/WALK-IN** Select some "high-energy" Christian music.
9:00 PM	**VIDEO** Show a sailing video. You can use the same one from the opening ceremonies or show different footage.
9:05 PM	**WELCOME/TOPIC INTRODUCTION** Host welcomes everyone and asks a few icebreaker questions to the audience, like: **How was dinner?** **Who has already unpacked?** **Which team will win competition this week?** He or she should then set up the evening's topic with a personal illustration such as how he or she became a Christian.
9:25 PM	**WORSHIP** Worship leader conducts 20 minutes of "up-tempo" celebrative-type songs. (See Appendix C for a list of choruses.)
9:45 PM	**MESSAGE–SETTING SAIL** See Evening Message #1 rationale and outline.
10:15 PM	**ANNOUNCEMENTS AND DISMISS** Host prays, gives the schedule for Day 2, and dismisses students to D-Team #2.

Big Idea

Do you remember how excited you were when you first came to Christ? You were probably ready to set off on a new voyage no matter how dangerous or rough. God has asked us to live our entire lives that way. What has happened? This message will help your students evaluate their spiritual journey.

Rationale

We can know where we are spiritually by examining one of four possible sailing situations:

- **On the Dock**–The student is not a Christian. He or she is not even in the boat.
- **Tied to the Dock**–The Christian student is pretending or "playing the Christian game." He or she is in the boat, but not doing anything to grow spiritually.
- **Dead in the Water**–The Christian student is in the boat out on the lake, but there is no wind in the sails. The boat does not seem to be going anywhere. The desire to "sail" is there, but perhaps the student feels stuck on a sandbar.
- **Sailing on Open Waters**–The Christian student is growing and developing a relationship with Jesus Christ. He or she is on the way to becoming a Fully Devoted Follower of Christ (FDF).

Message Outline

Let's take a closer look at each of these sailing situations.

I. On the Dock
a. What is life like on the dock?
1. No risk, no reward.
2. How can you say sailing is not for you if you've never been in the boat?

b. What does Jesus have to say to those on the dock?
1. Get off the dock. Read Acts 3:19.
2. Step in the boat. Read Matthew 4:19.

II. Tied to the Dock
a. What is life like for those tied to the dock?
1. Incomplete.
   - You get your feet wet, but that is all.
   - You come as far as the boat, but you have never sailed.
2. Indecisive.
   - It's time to shove off from the dock.
            or
   - It's time to get out of the boat.

b. What does Jesus have to say to those tied to the dock?
1. Come! Read Matthew 14:27-32.
2. Be either hot or cold. Read Revelation 3:16.

III. Dead in the Water
   a. What is life like for those dead in the water?
      1. Anxious.
         • Where has the wind gone?
         • How did I get here in the first place?
         • Why is everybody else around me sailing?
      2. Doubtful.
         • Why did I ever get in the boat?
         • Will I ever sail again?
   b. What does Jesus have to say to those dead in the water?
      1. Restore the joy of your salvation. Read Psalm 51:12.
      2. Raise your sails! Read John 3:8.

IV. Sailing on the Open Waters
   a. What is life like for those sailing on the open waters?
      1. Exciting.
         • You never know what is next. Read James 4:13-15.
         • Never lose the fervor. Read Romans 12:11.
      2. Secure.
         • You are sailing with the One who has the power to tell the wind and waves to be still. Read Matthew 8:23-27.
         • Hold on tight! Read Hebrews 10:23.
   b. What does Jesus have to say to those sailing on the open waters?
      1. Persevere. Read James 1:2-4.
      2. Throw off anything that would hinder. Read Hebrews 12:1.

V. Conclusion

When Hudson Taylor went to China, he made the voyage on a sailing vessel. As it neared the channel between the southern Malay Peninsula and the island of Sumatra, the missionary heard an urgent knock on his stateroom door. He opened it and there stood the captain of the ship.

"Mr. Taylor," he said, "we have no wind. We are drifting toward an island where the people are heathen and I fear they are cannibals."

"What can I do?" asked Taylor.

"I understand that you believe in God. I want you to pray for wind."

"All right, Captain, I will, but you must set the sail."

"Why that's ridiculous! There's not even the slightest breeze. Besides, the sailors will think I'm crazy."

But finally, because of Taylor's insistence, the captain agreed. Forty-five minutes later, he returned and found the missionary still on his knees. "You can stop praying now," said the captain. "We've got more wind than we know what to do with!"

It's time to raise the sail and join the adventure!

Day One
D-Team #2–Set Sail Walk

Objective

During this D-Team, you and your students will walk near the waterfront (if possible) in your camp and read four signs, which have been pre-set before this D-Team meets, at various stations. Remember to light the signs if this takes place at night. On each sign are the following descriptions:

- **On the Dock**–The student is not a Christian. He or she is not even in the boat.
- **Tied to the Dock**–The Christian student is pretending or "playing the Christian game." He or she is in the boat, but not doing anything to grow spiritually.
- **Dead in the Water**–The Christian student is in the boat out on the lake, but there is no wind in the sails. The boat does not seem to be going anywhere. The desire to "sail" is there, but perhaps the student feels stuck on a sandbar.
- **Sailing on Open Waters**–The Christian student who is growing and developing a relationship with Jesus Christ. He or she is on the way to becoming a Fully Devoted Follower of Christ (FDF).

Materials Needed

- Posterboard for signs and markers
- Copies of Set Sail Map (map of campsite depicting the four stations–see example on the following page)

Set Sail Map

Distribute the Set Sail Map to your students and explain that they will be using it for the next couple of days to determine the condition of their spiritual lives–where they are at, and where they are going. Next, have your students walk to each station and make sure they understand its significance. Ask your D-Team members if any of them are at that station in their lives. If so, then encourage them to take out their maps and have them sign their names at that particular station shown on the map. Continue until *everyone* has signed their maps.

In Closing

Close by praying for each person in your D-Team.

Evening Activity–Bonfire

After this D-Team, students may want to continue talking and sharing what they have learned. Build a bonfire somewhere on the campground. Bonfires create an atmosphere that facilitates talking and community building. Encourage your leaders to be strategic in using this time to invest in students. You may want to lead a short time of worship. Make sure you have marshmallows, chocolate, and graham crackers on hand for s'mores.

Set Sail Map

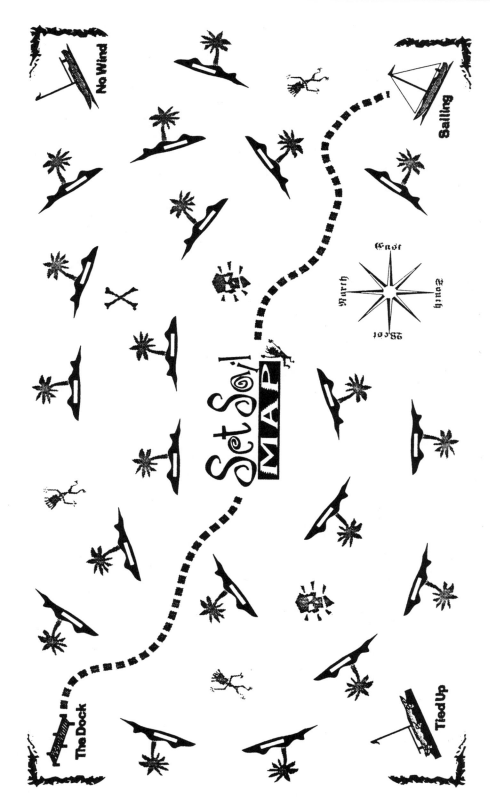

Day Two

Schedule

7:00 AM	Morning Worship
7:45 AM	Leaders' Meeting
8:00 AM	Breakfast
9:00 AM	Morning Session– **Rider of the Storm: Moses**
10:45 AM	Competition
12:30 PM	Lunch
1:30 PM	One-on-Ones
2:00 PM	Free Time
5:30 PM	Dinner
6:30 PM	D-Team #3– **Sailing Clothing**
8:30 PM	Evening Session– **Storms of Life**
9:30 PM	D-Team #4– **Islands of Safety**
10:30 PM	Movie and pizza
12:30 AM	Cabin Check
1:00 AM	Lights Out

Morning Worship

Student Notes #1 can be copied and highlighted ahead of time, before distributing it to your students and leaders. Highlight one line on each copy so that each person who receives a copy has a different line highlighted on his or her sheet. Then, when you ask for Psalm 104 to be read aloud, instruct those present to read aloud the lines that are highlighted on their sheet. Be prepared to fill in if someone misses his or her cue!

Program Cue Sheet

TIME	PROGRAM ELEMENT
7:45 AM	**LEADERS' MEETING** Student Minister
8:45 AM	**DOORS OPEN/WALK-IN** Play some "high-energy" Christian music.
9:00 AM	**ANNOUNCEMENTS** Host explains the rest of the day's schedule.
9:10 AM	**WORSHIP** Worship leader conducts 20 minutes of worship choruses focused on an attribute of God like His goodness.
9:30 AM	**DISMISS TO SITES FOR MORNING MESSAGES** Direct students to the four stations.
9:45 AM	**MORNING MESSAGE– RIDER OF THE STORM: MOSES** See Message #1 for rationale and outline.
10:15 AM	**PRAYER AND DISMISSAL TO COMPETITION** Give students time to go to their rooms and change for competition.

Morning Message # 1
Rider of the Storm: Moses

Big Idea
Often the storms in our lives come from our own failures. No matter how sincere our efforts, we sometimes still mess up. One of the greatest examples of God turning human failure into His success is found in the life of the legendary storm rider, Moses.

Rationale
Each of us can learn to weather the storms of life by learning three lessons from the failures and successes of Moses:
1. Don't forget to look up!
2. If you don't look up, you will go down!
3. Even if you go down, God can pick you up!

The Storm
Moses was a Hebrew by birth, but he grew up in the palace of Pharaoh. Every day, he saw his own people being beaten and oppressed by the Egyptians. Moses knew that God was calling him to do something about the plight of His people. The problem was that Moses acted out of his own strength and with his own plan. He didn't wait for God's direction! The result of this failure cost Moses years of separation from his people before God eventually used him to free Israel.

Message Outline

I. Don't Forget to Look Up!
   a. Moses saw an Egyptian slave master beating the Hebrew slave, one of his own countrymen. The Bible tells us that Moses looked "this way and that," but he never looked up. He never stopped to think or ask if this was God's way to go about freeing the nation of Israel (Exodus 2:11–14; Acts 7:23–25).
      1. When have you rushed into something before you stopped to ask God how He would want you to act?
      2. What causes you to try and act on your own instead of waiting for God to show His way? (Possible answers: impatience, anger, lack of prayer, greed.)
      3. What will help you to "look up" before you act on your own?

II. If You Don't Look Up, You Will Go Down!
   a. It is amazing to think that Moses could go so far as to murder someone. It is clear that when we persist in our own way, we are capable of making terrible mistakes. Moses paid a high price for his mistake. He spent 40 years as an alien in a foreign land, apart from his own people (Exodus 2:15–25; Acts 7:26–29).
      1. What has been the result of a time when you acted out of God's will?
      2. How did you feel when you realized what your mistake had cost you?
      3. How do you think Moses felt as he waited 40 years for God to restore him?
   b. Sometimes God allows us to suffer the consequences for our mistakes so that we can experience humility and learn that His way is always best.

III. Even If You Go Down, God Can Pick You Up!
   a. The final lesson we can learn from Moses is that even in the midst of the storms of our failures, God can still use us. Moses paid a high price, but he also learned a great lesson: It's never too late to "look up" (Exodus 3:7–10; 4:27–31; Acts 7:30–34).
      1. Has God ever used your mistakes to eventually achieve His purpose?
      2. Where is God currently trying to use you?
   b. Read Acts 7:35–36. When we learn to "look up," God shows us His way to weather the storms and uses us to do great things along the way!

Day Two-Competition
Volleyball Tournament

Depending on the size of your group, divide students into teams of two, four, or six. Two on two volleyball is more for advanced players, so teams of six would most likely be best. If time permits, allow each team to play one game against the rest of the teams (a round-robin format). Each game should be played to 15 points. You can determine the winning team by keeping track of each team's total points won or by the team who won the most games.

Equipment Needed: Volleyball net, volleyball, cones to mark court boundaries

Day Two
D-Team #3–Sailing Clothing

Objective
During this D-Team, you and your students will compare the importance of having the right clothing for sailing with the importance of putting on the armor of God.

Materials Needed
- Safety harness (safety line with a carabiner on each end)
- Life jacket
- Deck shoes (nonslip soles)
- Hat with visor
- Whistle
- Waterproof raincoat
- Copies of Student Notes #2

God's Clothing
Say: **The principal functions of sailing clothing are to help maintain body temperature, waterproof, and allow freedom of movement. This clothing is intended for long-distance and foul-weather sailing. Water and wind both contribute to loss of body heat, and modern sailing clothing helps protect the body. The materials used must be lightweight and quick-drying. The jacket should have numerous safety features, including life jacket, safety harness, whistle, and a pocket for emergency flares.**

Distribute copies of Student Notes #2. Then take each clothing item and pass it around the group. As you introduce each item, talk through the item's purpose and when each item would be useful to have ready.

Clothing Item	Purpose
Safety harness	In an emergency, attach one carabiner to a secure place on the boat and the other end to your jacket or lifejacket.
Life jacket	To keep a person afloat in the water.
Deck shoes	Nonslip-soled shoes worn so that when the deck is wet, a person can move around quickly without worrying about slipping overboard.
Hat with visor	Used to keep the sun and rain out of a person's eyes.
Whistle	Used when unsure if someone will see your boat due to storm or fog. Also used to let others know your general location.
Waterproof raincoat	Worn to keep a person dry.

Have one of your D-Team members read aloud Ephesians 6:10–17. Ask: **What is the theme of these verses? In what way does the theme of these verses relate to sailing clothing?**

Read the following Scriptures and discuss the following pieces of God's clothing:

- Belt of truth (John 8:31–32)
  How is the belt of truth like a safety harness? What is it, and how do we put on the belt of truth? (By acknowledging that Christ's teachings are the truth.)

- Breastplate of righteousness (Ephesians 6:14; Colossians 3:12–17)
  How is the breastplate of righteousness like a life jacket? What is the breastplate of righteousness, and how do we put it on? (By walking uprightly and godly.)

- Gospel of peace (Isaiah 52:7)
  How is the Gospel of peace like deck shoes? How do we apply this to our lives? (By standing firm in our faith, ready to proclaim the peace found in God.)

- Helmet of salvation (Exodus 15:2)
  How is the helmet of salvation like a hat with a visor? What is the helmet of salvation, and how do we use it? (By protecting our minds with God's truths to keep doubts from harming us.)

- Sword of the Spirit (John 15:26)
  How is the sword of the Spirit like a whistle? How can we use the sword of the Spirit daily? (By fighting the enemy with God's Word.)

- Shield of faith (Proverbs 3:5; Ephesians 6:16)
  How is the shield of faith like a waterproof raincoat? How can this shield protect us? (By preventing the enemy's flaming arrows–like temptation, discouragement, and doubt–from penetrating our hearts.)

In Closing
Share with your students that the evening message is on the storms of life and what was just studied will help us navigate through them. Close by praying for the person on your right.

Program Cue Sheet

TIME	PROGRAM ELEMENT
7:45 PM	**LEADERS' MEETING** Student Minister
8:15 PM	**DOORS OPEN/WALK-IN** Select some "high-energy" Christian music.
8:30 PM	**VIDEO** Show a video clip that shows footage of sailing through a storm.
8:35 PM	**WELCOME AND INTRODUCTION** Host shares a story of a storm that affected his or her life.
8:40 PM	**WORSHIP** Worship leader selects 15 minutes of songs focused on the power of God and His ability to sustain us through the various storms of life.
8:55 PM	**MESSAGE– STORMS OF LIFE** See Evening Message #2 for rationale and outline.
9:25 PM	**ANNOUNCEMENTS AND DISMISSAL** Host prays, gives the schedule for the next day, and dismisses students to D-Team #4.

Evening Message #2
Storms of Life

Big Idea
Life is rough for all of us at one time or another, and we all need some help in getting through those times. In this message, you will offer your students some hope and a few practical tools to weather the storms of life.

Rationale
We can know about the storms of life by looking at two kinds of storms found in the book of James (James 1:1–16):
Storm #1: Trials
Storm #2: Temptations

Message Outline
I. Trials
  a. What are they?
    1. The testing of one's faith (James 1:3).
    2. Share a personal story of how your faith was tested.
  b. What do they do?
    1. Develop perseverance (James 1:3).
    2. Share a personal story of how the testing of your faith developed perseverance.

II. Temptations
  a. What are they?
    1. Seductive suggestions to sin.
    2. Analogy of wanting something so badly that isn't good for you (James 1:14). Example: enticing of a chocolate bar.
  b. What do they do?
    1. Attempt to sever your relationship with God.
    2. When desire becomes reality, it leads to sin, which leads to death (James 1:15).
    3. Share a personal story of falling into temptation and the feelings of being separated from God.

III. So What Do I Do?
  a. Trials teach us to swim.
    1. Consider it pure joy. Why? Because God wants to develop perseverance in our lives (James 1:3).
    2. Let the trial finish its course. Why? So that we will be mature and not lacking anything (James 1:4).
    3. Wait for our crown of life. Why? Because God has promised a crown of life to those He loves who stand through the storms.
  b. Temptations cause us to drown.
    1. Realize God is not tempting us. Why? God cannot be tempted by evil and He does not tempt anyone (James 1:13).
    2. Don't let our desires conceive. Why? Because conception gives way to sin.
    3. Realize God is faithful. Why? He will not let us be tempted beyond what we can bear (1 Corinthians 10:13).
    4. There is a way out. How? God provides a way out so we can stand up under it (1 Corinthians 10:13).

Day Two
D-Team #4–Islands of Safety

Objective

In this D-Team, which follows Evening Message #2, you will explain how the storms in our lives cause us to be tossed about in the sea of life.

Materials Needed

- Set Sail map
- Colored markers

A Safe Haven

Emphasize that we need to find an island that will be a safe haven. Describe some possible islands that your students could sail to, but allow them to determine to which island they would like to sail. Use the following list to get them thinking:

Island of hope
Island of courage
Island of faith
Island of love
Island of accountability
Island of self-control
Island of happiness
Island of acceptance
Island of forgiveness
Island of ...

Display your Set Sail Map and have your students draw their boats somewhere on the sea, signifying that they are in a storm. Help your students define which island they are headed toward and then have them write the name of the island on it. Then have them draw a dotted line from their boat to the island that they have chosen.

In Closing

Have your students spend some time discussing how they plan to complete their voyage and what kind of help they might need. Ask God to help each person be courageous and faithful.

Evening Activity–Movie and Pizza

For this evening's activity, Student Impact served pizza and showed the movie *The Little Mermaid*, which fit well with the nautical theme.

Day Three

Schedule

7:00 AM	Morning Worship
7:45 AM	Leaders' Meeting
8:00 AM	Breakfast
9:00 AM	Morning Session– **Rider of the Storm: Gideon**
10:45 AM	Competition
12:30 PM	Lunch
1:30 PM	One-on-Ones
2:00 PM	Free Time
5:30 PM	Dinner
6:30 PM	D-Team #5– **First Things First**
8:30 PM	Evening Session– **Priorities: First Things First**
10:00 PM	D-Team #6– **Bowline Knot**
11:00 PM	Bonfire
12:30 AM	Cabin Check
1:00 AM	Lights Out

Morning Worship

Read or ask a student to read "The Choice" from Max Lucado's book *When God Whispers Your Name* (Word, 1994, pp. 73-74). Then spend some time in prayer, asking God to allow the fruit of the Spirit to be evident in each person's life that day.

Day Three
Morning Session #2

Program Cue Sheet

TIME	PROGRAM ELEMENT
7:45 AM	**LEADERS' MEETING** Student Minister
8:45 AM	**DOORS OPEN/WALK-IN** Play some "high-energy" Christian music.
9:00 AM	**ANNOUNCEMENTS** Host explains the rest of the day's schedule.
9:10 AM	**WORSHIP** Worship leader conducts 20 minutes of worship choruses focused on an attribute of God, like His love.
9:30 AM	**DISMISS TO SITES FOR MORNING MESSAGES** Direct students to the four stations.
9:45 AM	**MORNING MESSAGE– RIDER OF THE STORM: GIDEON** See Message #2 for rationale and outline.
10:15 AM	**PRAYER AND DISMISSAL TO COMPETITION** Give students time to go to their rooms and change for competition.

Morning Message #2
Rider of the Storm: Gideon

Big Idea

In the book of Judges, we read of a man named Gideon who was able to weather a terrible storm and restore peace to the Israelites, God's chosen people. When the Lord appeared to Gideon and told him how he could end the oppression of the Israelites, Gideon must have thought God was kidding. Yet, in the end, Gideon trusted and was able to conquer.

Rationale

Each one of us can learn to ride out the storms of our lives by asking the same three questions Gideon asked:

1. Who am I, God?
2. Who are You, God?
3. What should I do, God?

The Storm

The Israelites had settled into the Promised Land, and the covenants God had made in the desert were now fulfilled. The book of Judges deals with the pattern of the Israelites losing sight of the covenants God had made with them in the past, and instead clinging to Canaan's earthly rules, beliefs, and kings. When things got really bad, the Israelites would inevitably cry to God for help. Time and again, God raised up leaders (judges) through whom He restored peace.

Gideon was one of these judges. The Israelites had forgotten God's promises and they had done "evil in the eyes of the LORD" (Judges 6:1). Because they worshiped kings instead of God, they suffered greatly. The Midianites had been attacking, stealing, and oppressing the Israelites for seven years. As the cycle goes in the book of Judges, the Israelites

again cried out for help (Judges 6:6–7). The Lord answered by appearing to Gideon and telling him to rise up and save Israel. Gideon was shocked, but because he asked three very important questions, he was able to weather an incredible storm.

Message Outline

I. Who Am I, God?
   a. Read Judges 6:11–16. The Lord spoke with Gideon and even called him a "mighty warrior" (6:12). Yet, Gideon had self-doubt. It was hard for him to obey God because he wasn't confident in his human strength. Have you ever doubted your own abilities even though you knew God supported you? When did this happen? Why do you think it happened?
   b. Most of us would agree that we would rather be one person fighting with God than one billion people fighting without God. Then why do we so often choose the side without God? Even when God promised to help Gideon strike down the Midianites (6:16), did Gideon give an immediate yes to God?
   c. After Gideon got over his self-doubt, what were his new concerns? (Gideon went from questioning his own abilities to questioning God's.)

II. Who Are You, God?
   Judges 6:17–40–Gideon then turned to questioning God. It is easy to see why Gideon might have needed reassurance that he was really talking

to God. After all, idol worship was rampant and Gideon wanted to be sure he wasn't listening to an "impostor." However, this does not mean it was okay for Gideon to "put God to the test." As believers, we live and die by our faith.

- Would you have been able to take this step of faith with God without having proof that it was really Him?
- Has there been a time in your life when you feel you have trusted God without first questioning whether it was really God prompting you?
- What was the first test that Gideon offered? (6:19) What was the result? (He made an offering of goat and unleavened bread. An angel of the Lord turned the meat and bread into fire.)
- Read Judges 6:36–40. What was the second test Gideon placed before God? (He asked God to put dew on the fleece, but keep the remaining ground dry.)
- What was the last test? (He asked God to leave the fleece dry, but put dew on the rest of the ground.)
- What is the fleece in your life? What are you waiting for God to prove to you before you will fully obey Him?

III. What Should I Do, God?
Judges 7:1–25–Finally we reach the most important and only question that really needs to be answered in order to weather any storm. However, we often need the confidence that comes from answering the first two questions before we can do anything for and with God. Gideon was now at the point where he would do exactly what God asked no matter what the cost. What a great place to be!

- Have you ever been able to say to God, "Whatever you say, Master?"
- What were the circumstances that eventually led to Gideon's defeat of the Midianites? (7:1–25)
- Once Gideon was secure in his own strength and sure he was really dealing with God, did he have any second thoughts or doubts? (No!)

IV. Conclusion
When we know who we are as children of God and who God is in our lives, then we can have the strength to ride out any storms that cross our paths.

Tug-of-war

Determine the strongest team in your ministry by playing tug-of-war. Use a long, strong rope (50 ft. in length) and place a team at each end of the rope (teams can range from 6–15 students). Tie a bandana in the center of the rope and mark boundaries one foot from either side of the bandana. When the whistle blows, each team tries to pull the opposing team past their boundary line and onto their side. You can organize teams according to campus, year in school (freshmen vs. freshmen), students vs. leaders, guys vs. guys, or girls vs. girls. If your group is large, have several ropes so many students can play at the same time.

Slip n' Slide Contest

Find a 4 ft. x 30 ft. sheet of plastic. Hose down the plastic with water and then pour some dish soap and/or baby oil onto the plastic. Hold a "slip n' slide" contest for distance, form, and originality.

Day Three
D-Team #5–First Things First

Objective
In this D-Team, you will stress the importance of determining priorities in life.

Materials Needed
- Logbooks
- Pens

A Lively Crew of Sailors
The following story will help your students begin thinking about priorities. You will challenge them to write down some priorities in their own lives. Inform them that you are going to tell them a story about your D-team and an adventure that took a bad turn. They will need to be prepared to make some quick decisions on their own and then together. Read aloud:

There once was a boat named
_____ and it had a lively crew of sailors whose names were
_____. They sailed out one fine afternoon with high hopes of discovering new land. The weather was great for the first few days, but then the skies blackened and the waves rose quite dangerously. Then the storm hit. It was the worst storm the captain had ever seen in (his/her) lifetime. The captain gathered (his/her) crew together and informed them that their chances of survival were not looking good. So they needed to make a decision–should they go down with the ship or try to make it in the life raft? It was unanimously decided that they would attempt survival in the small raft. There wasn't much time left before their ship would begin to break up. The captain instructed them

to only take 10 items with them onto the raft. They had to make their choices quickly. They would meet back on deck within 10 minutes and load the raft.

Distribute copies of Student Notes #3 and send your students out for 10 minutes to choose ten possible items from the list shown below that could be taken on the life raft:

Rope	Helmet
Anchor	Hourglass
Fishing Pole	Knife
Compass	Leak Stopper
Magnifying Glass	Flashlight
Oars	Boots
Air Pump	Water Supply
Emergency Kit	Charcoal
Life Jackets	Hand Warmer
Raft Repair Kit	Zinc Cream
Anti-seasickness Band	Whistle
Fog Horn	Ship's Bell
Binoculars	Wardrobe
Buoys	Video Camera
Carabiner	Ladder
Map	Camera
Direction Locator	Tools
Diver's Equipment	Suspenders
Epoxy Resin	Mirror
Flare Gun (with flares)	Sundial
Telescope	Radio

After 10 minutes, call the group back together and continue the story:

The crew met back on deck 10 minutes later and began to load the small raft with all the items that they had quickly gathered. But it became

obvious that the crew and all their gear were not going to be able to fit, much less float! So, the captain halted the loading and decided that they needed to consolidate what would be allowed on the raft with them–everything else must perish with the ship. Each of the crew members began to list off what they felt was important and the captain started a master list of what was similarly important to all.

Have your students read their lists and write down the similar items that are read. Then continue your story.

There were sacrifices to be made but they all knew it had to be done. They decided that only 10 total items could be carried onto the raft with them if

they wanted even half a chance of surviving. Thus, the list began to be revised.

Have your students work on their list and choose 10 total items to take on the raft. Then discuss the importance of having priorities and focusing on what is key in our lives. Give them some time to write down 10 priorities in their lives, and then number them according to importance.

In Closing

Share with your students that they will be learning about how God fits into our priorities in Evening Message #3. Suggest that they keep their lists handy so that they can apply what is taught. Spend some time praying for each other before you dismiss.

Day Three
Evening Session #3

Program Cue Sheet

TIME	PROGRAM ELEMENT
7:45 PM	**LEADERS' MEETING** Student Minister
8:15 PM	**DOORS OPEN/WALK-IN** Select some "high-energy" Christian music.
8:30 PM	**WELCOME AND TOPIC INTRODUCTION** Host share a personal story about having the right priorities or what it's like to have your priorities out of order.
8:40 PM	**WORSHIP** Worship leader conducts 10 minutes worth of "up-tempo" celebrative choruses.
8:50 PM	**VIDEO** Play a video or audio interview of a student sharing his or her story of how he or she attempted to find purpose and clarity in life. Or ask a student to share his or her story "live."
9:00 PM	**WORSHIP** Worship leader conducts 15 minutes of choruses that focus on living fully for Christ.
9:15 PM	**MESSAGE–PRIORITIES: FIRST THINGS FIRST** See Evening Message #3 rationale and outline.
9:45 PM	**ANNOUNCEMENTS AND DISMISS** Host prays, gives the schedule for the next day, and dismisses students to D-Team #6.

Evening Message #3
Priorities: First Things First

Big Idea
Most of us are always looking for new ways to maintain order in our lives. In this message, you will provide some practical ways God desires that we organize our lives.

Rationale
We can know how to have a well-ordered life by adopting two important life principles:

    Principle #1: Know our purpose
    Principle #2: Prioritize–first things first

Message Outline
I. Know Your Purpose
    a. You have been given a purpose by God Himself (Jeremiah 29:11).
    b. We all share one purpose (Luke 10:27).
    c. We all have individual purposes (Ephesians 2:10).

II. Prioritize
    a. Community
        • Importance of community (Hebrews 10:25).
        • Life in community (Acts 2:42–47).
    b. Evangelism
        • Be ready to do the work (2 Timothy 4:2–5).
        • Go and make disciples (Matthew 28:19–20).
    c. Disciplines
        • Prayer (Ephesians 6:18).
        • Solitude (Matthew 14:23).
        • Scripture reading (Psalm 119:11).

Objective

In this D-Team, you will stress the need to have a tight relationship with Jesus Christ in order to maintain consistency in our priorities. In this session, you will be teaching your students how to tie the knot most often used by sailors because it is the strongest knot–as long as there is tension between the two ends. On the other hand, if there is not tension, this knot is one of the easiest to untie. It is called the bowline knot. Be sure to read the following instructions and practice tying the knot several times prior to this D-Team.

Instructions for Tying a Bowline Knot

1. Take the rope in your right hand and make a loop. This is called "the hole."
2. The end of the rope on top going away from you is called "the rabbit."
3. The end of the rope on the bottom coming toward you is called "the tree."
4. Take the rabbit and come up out of the hole, leaving a small loop hanging out of the hole.
5. Next take the rabbit around the tree and then back through the hole.
6. Lastly, pull on the rabbit and tree to finish your bowline knot.

Materials Needed

- a piece of rope for each student
- priority lists from D-Team #5

Keeping the Tension

Have your students pull out their priority lists from the last D-Team experience.

Ask: **How does God play a part in your priorities? What, if anything, would you change now that you have heard Evening Message #3?**

Ask your students if they want Christ to be the Person holding the other end of the rope that is wrapped around the things that are most important to them. If a student answers yes, then help him or her tie the bowline knot. As your students are pulling the "rabbit and the tree" tight, let them know that they are in essence saying that they are committed to keeping their relationship with Jesus Christ tight.

In Closing

Pray with each student, or have the whole group circle around and pray for that person. Then continue until each student has had the chance to tie his or her bowline knot. If some of your students are not ready to make that commitment or need time to think things over, be sensitive and plan to talk with them one-on-one.

Evening Activity: Bonfire

Because D-Team #6 is scheduled so late at night, some students may finish their D-Team experiences and go to their cabins. For others, you may want to build another bonfire to give students time to continue building relationships. At this point in camp, students probably have built deeper friendships and feel connected to others. This evening activity will give them time to talk further with friends and just "hang out." Memories that will never be forgotten are made around the campfire.

Day Four

Schedule

7:00 AM	Morning Worship
7:45 AM	Leaders' Meeting
8:00 AM	Breakfast
9:00 AM	Morning Session– **Rider of the Storm: Noah**
10:45 AM	Competition
12:30 PM	Lunch
1:30 PM	One-on-Ones
2:00 PM	Free Time
5:30 PM	Dinner
6:30 PM	D-Team #7– **Signal Flags**
8:30 PM	Evening Session– **Nail Your Colors**
10:30 PM	Concert of Prayer
12:30 AM	Cabin Check
1:00 AM	Lights Out

Morning Worship

Use Steve Camp's song, "Whatever You Ask," *(Doing My Best,* Sparrow, 1990) to start this morning's worship. After the song, break into groups of three or four and encourage your students and leaders to spend some time submitting their hearts to God. Ask them to commit to doing whatever God asks of them throughout the day.

Program Cue Sheet

TIME	PROGRAM ELEMENT
7:45 AM	**LEADERS' MEETING** Student Minister
8:45 AM	**DOORS OPEN/WALK-IN** Play some "high-energy" Christian music.
9:00 AM	**ANNOUNCEMENTS** Host explains the rest of the day's schedule.
9:10 AM	**WORSHIP** Worship leader conducts 20 minutes of worship choruses focused on an attribute of God, like His faithfulness.
9:30 AM	**DISMISS TO SITES FOR MORNING MESSAGES** Direct students to the four stations.
9:45 AM	**MORNING MESSAGE– RIDER OF THE STORM: NOAH** See Message #3 for rationale and outline.
10:15 AM	**PRAYER AND DISMISSAL TO COMPETITION** Give students time to go to their rooms and change for competition.

Morning Message #3
Rider of the Storm: Noah

Big Idea
Sometimes when the storms of life hit us, we feel alone. We can be encouraged by the legendary storm rider, Noah. He was called by God during a storm to stand alone and stand strong.

Rationale
Each one of us can learn to ride out the storms in our lives with God by learning three lessons from the life of Noah. We must
1. Stand
2. Obey
3. Wait

The Storm
God was about to destroy the entire earth! He was going to wipe out all living things because of their sinfulness. Genesis 6:5 describes just how evil people had become. In Genesis 6:6, we read that God was grieved that He had ever created humans! Only Noah was chosen to be spared because "Noah was a righteous man, blameless among the people of his time, and he walked with God" (Genesis 6:9). God singled out Noah and chose to make a new start with him. Can you imagine how scared Noah must have been? No one had ever even seen an ark before, much less built one! This was a huge burden for one man and his family to carry. Only through Noah's willingness to stand with God, obey God, and wait for God was it possible to weather the storm.

Message Outline
I.   Stand Strong Even When Those Around You Are Falling!
   a. Genesis 6:11–13–Noah was alone in his righteousness.
- He walked with God even though everybody around him was corrupt.
- When have you felt alone in your walk with God? In your desire to pursue righteousness?

   b. Romans 12:2–It was not easy for Noah to stay a righteous man when everyone and everything around him was evil.
- God has called us to be different, to stand out because we have chosen to follow him and not the world. Sometimes we might even be left standing all alone.
- Do you ever find yourself giving in to sin because you rationalize that if everyone around you is doing it, how can it be wrong? What are some of the sins that tempt you?
- What would help you to stand?

II. Obey God Immediately Even in the Little Things in Your Life.
Genesis 6:14-22; 7:1-5–"Noah did everything just as God commanded him." God's instructions sounded ludicrous, but Noah obeyed.
- We are sometimes tempted to try and obey God in certain areas and not obey Him in others. But God calls us to absolute obedience with

our lives. It is the only way we can stand strong in the storms of life.

- Noah's faith in God made him obey.
- In what areas of your life do you struggle to obey God? Share a personal story from your own life.

III. Wait Patiently for God's Timing and Direction.
Genesis 8:1–22–"Noah waited." It is easy to want to rush in and try to do it all ourselves. Noah, however, waited for God to make it clear (Genesis 8:15–16).

- God made a covenant with Noah. He promised never to destroy all earthly life with a natural catastrophe again. The covenant sign would be a rainbow.
- When has it been hard for you to wait on God? Share a personal story from your own life.
- Can you think of a time when your willingness to wait on God brought you rewards?

IV. Conclusion
When we wait for God's direction, we can see clearly how to ride out the storm.

Competition

Bellyflop and Diving Contest

At the pool or lake, ask a representative (or one guy and one girl) from each campus team to perform the best possible bellyflop. Have a panel of judges hold up cards ranging from 1 to 10 to score each contestant. Then find a different representative to perform: the most original dive, the most difficult dive, or the funniest dive. The judges should again score each diver. Make sure the water where the diving will take place is suitable for diving and that a lifeguard is present. Think about safety for this competition and do not take any risks.

Day Four
D-Team #7–Signal Flags

Objective

You have just spent three days digging into your students' lives and finding out a little more about who they are. Tonight will be the compilation of everything that they have learned about themselves and their relationship with Christ. For centuries, flags of different decorations, designs, and colors have been used to identify ships. Each signal flag or combination of flags had a different meaning. In this D-Team, your students will design a flag by using different colored crayons and drawing symbols that represent who they are.

Materials Needed

- Flags–2' x 2' pieces of material or tagboard. You can purchase inexpensive, flat white sheets and cut several flags out of each sheet.
- Crayons or markers

Flagging

Before your students design their flags, review the D-Team experiences that your students have participated in over the past few days. Highlight any defining moments that have occurred in the life of each student. Have them write down the things that you point out about them that they can use to create their flags. Hand out the flags and the crayons and then give them these guidelines: **Make your flag a positive representation of who you are by using colors or symbols. Write what each color represents for you on the back of your flag. Then plan to bring your flag to Evening Message #4.**

Day Four
Evening Session #4

Program Cue Sheet

TIME	PROGRAM ELEMENT
7:45 PM	**LEADERS' MEETING** Student Minister
8:15 PM	**DOORS OPEN/WALK-IN** Select some "high-energy" Christian music.
8:30 PM	**VIDEO** Show highlights from the week of camp. If you have not videotaped the camp activities, have a leader and/or student share some fun stories and recap the highlights of the week.
8:45 PM	**WELCOME AND TOPIC INTRODUCTION** Host shares a personal story about following and obeying Christ.
9:00 PM	**WORSHIP** Worship leader conducts 20 minutes of choruses that focus on being committed to honoring God with our lives.
9:20 PM	**MESSAGE—NAIL YOUR COLORS** See Evening Message #4 rationale and outline.
10:00 PM	**SONG** Select a contemporary Christian song about living for Christ.

10:05 PM **ANNOUNCEMENTS AND DISMISS**
Host prays and gives the schedule for the Concert of Prayer.

Evening Message #4
Nail Your Colors

Big Idea
During the Battle of Lake Erie in the War of 1812, a dying naval officer told his shipmates, "Don't give up the ship!" A flag with this saying was made and the crew "nailed" their colors (unit flag) on the mast of the ship to symbolize their commitment, loyalty, and willingness to die for their country. In the same way, Christ allowed Himself to be nailed to the cross as a sign of His commitment and loyalty to be obedient to His Father. As Christians, we have been commanded to remember the sacrifice that was made for us—Christ's death. In this message, you will encourage your students to remember and recommit themselves to Christ. Plan to end your message with the students nailing the colored flags they have made in D-Team #7 to a cross or flagpole.

Rationale
We can begin or continue to "set sail" in our spiritual lives by nailing our colors and declaring our commitment to Christ.

Message Outline
I.   Introduction—Navy Story.
   a. Their flag represented their loyalty and commitment.
   b. Their commitment was even unto death.

II. Our Flags.
   a. Read Luke 9:23–26 and emphasize that we need to take a stand for Christ.
   b. What does your flag represent?

III. Our Commitment to God.
   a. What do you want to declare to God? What are you willing to commit to Him?
   b. What do you want to declare to others? Give students (who are willing to share) the opportunity to publicly share their declaration with the entire group.
   c. Ask students, who are ready and willing, to "nail" their flags to the flagpole or cross. Do not force anyone to make a commitment; it must be each student's choice. Some students may not be ready to fully commit to God.
   d. Gather the group around the pole or cross and close in prayer.

Evening Activity: Concert of Prayer
A concert of prayer is a powerful and meaningful activity to have on the last night of camp. It gives students more time to focus solely on God and all that they have learned about Him during the week. Remember that this follows the message in which students "nailed their colors" and took a stand for Christ. Hearts will probably be tender after such a moment, so be sure to include some time for quiet reflection and individual prayer. The concert of prayer should also include corporate prayer, Scripture reading, worship, and communion. The student minister and worship leader should lead students during this time. Communion should be given according to the theology and traditions of your church or organization.

Day Five

Schedule

7:00 AM	Morning Worship
7:45 AM	Leaders' Meeting
8:00 AM	Breakfast
9:00 AM	Morning Session– **Rider of the Storm: Abraham**
10:45 AM	Competition
12:30 PM	Lunch
1:30 PM	Pack and Clean Cabins
2:30 PM	Closing Ceremonies
3:00 PM	Load Buses
5:00 PM	Dinner Break
6:00 PM	Load Buses for Last Leg of Trip

Morning Worship

Spend your last morning together sharing stories of how God worked in peoples' lives during the week. Encourage as many students and leaders as possible to share one or two lessons God taught them or one new truth with which they will leave camp. Spend time praying, thanking God for the incredible ways He touched hearts. Claim the following promise and remind students and leaders that "he who began a good work in you will carry it on to completion until the day of Christ Jesus" (Philippians 1:6).

Program Cue Sheet

TIME	PROGRAM ELEMENT
7:45 AM	**LEADERS' MEETING** Student Minister
8:45 AM	**DOORS OPEN/WALK-IN** Play some "high-energy" Christian music.
9:00 AM	**ANNOUNCEMENTS** Host explains the rest of the day's schedule.
9:10 AM	**WORSHIP** Worship leader conducts 20 minutes of worship choruses focused on God's trustworthiness.
9:30 AM	**DISMISS TO SITES FOR MORNING MESSAGES** Direct students to the four stations.
9:45 AM	**MORNING MESSAGE– RIDER OF THE STORM: ABRAHAM** See Message #4 for rationale and outline.
10:15 AM	**PRAYER AND DISMISSAL TO COMPETITION** Give students time to go to their rooms and change for competition.

Morning Message #4
Rider of the Storm: Abraham

Big Idea

Storms can be very long or at least seem that way. In this message, you will give your students some encouragement by telling them the story of Abraham.

Rationale

We should be able to navigate the storms of life by using three faith builders:

- Remembering God's faithfulness.
- Trusting God's faithfulness.
- Following God faithfully.

The Storm

The Holocaust Museum in Washington, D.C., serves as a living memorial to all those who survived and died in the Holocaust. Upon entering the museum, you are given a card with the identity of a Holocaust victim. You then walk through an actual boxcar which carried the victims to the concentration camps, see the actual camp bunk beds, and walk by piles and piles of shoes and hair. Before you know it, four hours have passed and the tour ends with a video of survivors telling their stories. Every one of their stories had one thing in common: These victims survived the horror of the Holocaust by having faith.

Few of us will ever go through a storm as devastating as the Holocaust, but all of us will encounter storms of our own. Whether those storms will be storms of divorce, death, or even fights with a boyfriend or girlfriend, we all need to be prepared to ride through them.

Message Outline

I. Introduction

We are going to look at the life of a Rider of the Storm. His name is Abraham and he is hailed throughout the Old and New Testaments as being a man of faith. Ask students to think about the person they love most. One of Abraham's greatest loves was his only son, Isaac. Listen to how Abraham rode the storm when his faith was tested.

a. Read Genesis 22:1–10. Ask: **Can you imagine being asked to put the one you love most to death? How would you respond?**

b. Look again at verse 5. Abraham believed that God would some how take care of Isaac. As we look at one of the storms in Abraham's life, you will see that every one of us should be able to navigate the storms of life by learning about three faith builders:

- Remember God's faithfulness.
- Trust God's faithfulness.
- Follow God faithfully.

II. Remember God's Faithfulness.

a. God's faithfulness to Abraham.
- God's covenant with Abraham.
- God's promise to Abraham (Genesis 12:1–4).
- Abraham remembered God's promise by building an altar (Genesis 12:6).

b. God's faithfulness to you.
Ask: **Do you have a story to remind you of God's faithfulness to you?** Think of an example from your life to share.

III. Trust God's Faithfulness.
    a. Abraham and Sarah
       (Genesis 17:1–8, 15–19; 21:1)
       trusted God.
       • God promised that they would
         have a son even though they
         were very old.
       • They continued to trust God,
         and Isaac was born
         (Genesis 21:1).
    b. God is trustworthy.
       • How has God shown you that
         He is trustworthy? Think of an
         example from your life to share
         about why you trust God.

IV. Follow God Faithfully.
    a. Abraham lived by faith until he
       died.
       • Read Romans 4:18–21 (Paul's
         description of Abraham).
    b. God is worth following. Think of
       an example from your life to share
       why you follow God.

V. Conclusion
Have the students write the word
remember on their shoes, hands,
arms, etc. Instruct them that during
their next quiet time, they should ask
God to help them remember a time
when He was faithful to them. Then
they should do something to remember, like tie a string around their fin-
ger or do what Abraham did–build an
altar. Remind them that when the
storms come, they can trust that God
will be faithful again and follow Him.

Swim Relays and Canoe Races

At the pool or lake, establish the distance for the swim relay. Six students should be on each relay team. When the whistle blows, the first team member swims to the designated point and back, tagging the next team member. The team that finishes first wins. If space permits, five or six teams can swim at the same time. If canoes are available, organize canoe races. Be extra careful around the waterfront and make sure a lifeguard is on duty.

 # Closing Ceremonies

After students finish packing, bring everyone together for a brief closing ceremony before boarding the buses. Meet around the flagpole where your flags are still flying. Student Impact fired a cannon and announced the competition team winner for the week. Offer a prayer of thanksgiving for God's goodness during the week. After praying, encourage students to find their flags and take them home.

Camp Follow-up

- Show pictures or video highlights of the camp at your next student program.
- Follow up on new students who came to camp and make sure they stay connected in the ministry.
- Follow up immediately on students who made decisions to trust Christ.
- Use the momentum of camp and keep building on it by meeting together on a regular basis.
- Continue teaching topics related to the camp theme of sailing and storms of life.
- Encourage leaders to continue building relationships with the students in their small groups and to check on areas in which students committed to grow.
- Provide opportunities for students to maintain the bonds they built by implementing or continuing a small group ministry and placing students on campus teams.
- Evaluate the camp by asking the following questions:
  Did the facility serve us well?
  Would we go there again?
  Did we promote camp far enough in advance?
  How did students respond to the speaker?
  Would we ask him or her to speak at next year's camp?
  Did the programming elements flow together smoothly?
  How did we do financially? Do we need to budget more money next year?
  Was the schedule too packed or was there the right amount of free time?
  Did we have the right leaders and enough volunteers to help?
  What did we learn?
  How can next year's camp be better?
- Write thank-you notes to your leaders, speaker, and musicians.
- Call or write the campsite and thank the personnel for their help in making your camp run smoothly.
- Take time to celebrate with your staff and/or leadership team the amazing things God did at the camp.
- Rest!

Student Notes # I
Psalm 104

If you have been asked to read the section of Psalm 104 highlighted on this page, then be prepared to stand and read it when your turn comes.

Otherwise, relax, look around, and enjoy the beauty of God's creation while the psalm is being read.

Praise the LORD, O my soul.
O LORD my God, you are very great;
you are clothed with splendor and majesty.
He wraps himself in light as with a garment;
he stretches out the heavens like a tent and lays the beams of his upper chambers on their waters.
He makes the clouds his chariot and rides on the wings of the wind.
He makes winds his messengers, flames of fire his servants.
He set the earth on its foundations; it can never be moved.
You covered it with the deep as with a garment; the waters stood above the mountains.
But at your rebuke the waters fled, at the sound of your thunder they took to flight;
they flowed over the mountains, they went down into the valleys, to the place you assigned for them.
You set a boundary they cannot cross; never again will they cover the earth.
He makes springs pour water into the ravines; it flows between the mountains.
They give water to all the beasts of the field; the wild donkeys quench their thirst.
The birds of the air nest by the waters; they sing among the branches.
He waters the mountains from his upper chambers; the earth is satisfied by the fruit of his work.
He makes grass grow for the cattle, and plants for man to cultivate–bringing forth food from the earth:
wine that gladdens the heart of man, oil to make his face shine, and bread that sustains his heart.
The trees of the LORD are well watered, the cedars of Lebanon that he planted.
There the birds make their nests; the stork has its home in the pine trees.
The high mountains belong to the wild goats; the crags are a refuge for the coneys.
The moon marks off the seasons, and the sun knows when to go down.
You bring darkness, it becomes night, and all the beasts of the forest prowl.
The lions roar for their prey and seek their food from God.
The sun rises, and they steal away; they return and lie down in their dens.
Then man goes out to his work, to his labor until evening.
How many are your works, O LORD!
In wisdom you made them all; the earth is full of your creatures.
There is the sea, vast and spacious, teeming with creatures beyond number–living things both large and small.
There the ships go to and fro, and the leviathan, which you formed to frolic there.
These all look to you to give them their food at the proper time.
When you give it to them, they gather it up; when you open your hand, they are satisfied with good things.
When you hide your face, they are terrified; when you take away their breath, they die and return to the dust.
When you send your Spirit, they are created, and you renew the face of the earth.
May the glory of the LORD endure forever; may the LORD rejoice in his works–
He who looks at the earth, and it trembles, who touches the mountains, and they smoke.
I will sing to the LORD all my life;
I will sing praise to my God as long as I live.
May my meditation be pleasing to him as I rejoice in the LORD.
But may sinners vanish from the earth and the wicked be no more.
Praise the LORD, O my soul.
Praise the LORD.

Student Notes #2
Sailing Clothing

Clothing Item	Purpose
Safety harness	
Life jacket	
Deck shoes	
Hat with visor	
Whistle	
Waterproof raincoat	

Read Ephesians 6:10–17. What is the theme of these verses? In what way does the theme of these verses relate to sailing clothing?

Read the following Scriptures and discuss the following pieces of God's clothing:

• Belt of truth (John 8:31–32) What is the belt of truth, and how do we put it on? How is the belt of truth like a safety harness?

• Breastplate of righteousness (Ephesians 6:14; Colossians 3:12–17) What is the breastplate of righteousness, and how do we put it on? How is the breastplate of righteousness like a life jacket?

• Gospel of peace (Isaiah 52:7) How is the Gospel of peace like deck shoes? How do we apply this to our lives?

• Helmet of salvation (Exodus 15:2) How is the helmet of salvation like a hat with a visor?

• Sword of the Spirit (John 15:26) How is the sword of the Spirit like a whistle? How can we use the sword of the Spirit daily?

• Shield of faith (Proverbs 3:5; Ephesians 6:16) How is the shield of faith like a waterproof raincoat? How can this shield protect us?

First Things First

List of possible items that could be taken on the life raft:

Rope	Helmet	Anchor	Hourglass
Fishing Pole	Knife	Compass	Leak Stopper
Flashlight	Magnifying Glass	Oars	Boots
Air Pump	Water Supply	Emergency Kit	Charcoal
Life Jackets	Hand Warmer	Raft Repair Kit	Zinc Cream
Anti-seasickness Band	Whistle	Fog Horn	Ship's Bell
Binoculars	Wardrobe	Buoys	Video Camera
Carabiner	Ladder	Map	Camera
Direction Locator	Tools	Diver's Equipment	Suspenders
Epoxy Resin	Mirror	Flare Gun (with flares)	Sundial
	Telescope	Radio	

Top 10 items I would take in the life raft:

1.
2.
3.
4.
5.
6.
7.
8.
9.
10.

Circle the above items that became a part of your D-Team's final top 10 items.

Top 10 priorities in my life:

1.
2.
3.
4.
5.
6.
7.
8.
9.
10.

IMPACT

Camp Summary: This camp* is an opportunity to teach your core students about your ministry and its vision for the coming season. Students will be "accepted" into the university upon registration and "graduate" by the end of the camp with excitement and a clear vision for your ministry season.

Length of Camp: Four days.

Target Audience: Christian students who desire to grow in their faith and become committed participants in building your student ministry.

Facility Requirements: A cabin or retreat center.

Camp Objectives:

- To challenge each student to take an active role in building your student ministry.
- To train and build a student core who understands your ministry's philosophy.
- To build relationships and unity among students.
- To give leaders opportunities to invest in the lives of students.

*We called this camp Impact University to reflect the name of our student ministry: Student Impact. We encourage you to adapt the name and "U" logo to fit your own ministry (e.g., Sonlight U, Logos U, etc.).

 Introduction

When was the last time you finished something–endured and saw it out until the end? For example, do you remember finishing your senior year of high school? How did you feel at graduation? If you're like most people, you felt great! The graduation ceremony marked a level of educational achievement for you personally. You walked away with a diploma that reminded you of that journey and encouraged you to continue to learn throughout your life.

At times, all of us find ourselves in a ministry "rut"–doing the same things because that's what we've always done. We develop an attitude of maintenance or preservation toward our ministry, forgetting the excitement of the "new."

This retreat is a four-day camp program with a college theme–Impact University. The theme focuses on a learning atmosphere where you can present your student ministry's vision, mission, and strategy to your students and leaders. It also serves as a great place for you to unveil a new direction or structural changes for the ministry. You will get a clearer picture of how to coordinate the programming elements, messages, competitions, and small groups on these next pages.

You will be emphasizing the value that your student ministry is focused on individuals, not numbers. In other words, everything that is said and done over the next four days will be focused on ministering to each student. The phrase "Just For You" is one that students and leaders can hold on to throughout the ministry year.

Camp Checklist

ACTIVITIES/TEAM BUILDERS
___ Elements for communion
___ An old king-size bedsheet

COMPETITION
___ Equipment for cross camp race (See page 95.)
___ Volleyball and volleyball net

D-TEAMS
___ Recording of "The Mountain" by Steven Curtis Chapman (*Heaven in the Real World*, Sparrow, 1994)
___ A watch
___ Tape/CD player

EMERGENCIES
___ First Aid Kit
___ Names and phone numbers of each camper's parent or guardian
___ Name and directions to nearest hospital from campsite

HANDOUTS AND SUPPLIES
___ Student notebooks
___ Copies of Student Notes #1, #2, #3, #4, and #5
___ Leader Responsibility Sheets
___ Extra Bibles
___ Camera and/or video

PROGRAMS
___ Musical instruments
___ Props for stage
___ "Pomp & Circumstance" music
___ Walk-in music as students enter program
___ Song sheets or slides for worship choruses

REGISTRATION
___ Completed permission slips from each camper and leader
___ Room assignments
___ Petty cash box to collect remaining payments for camp

VEHICLES
___ Maps to campsite
___ Insurance documents
___ Money for gas and tolls

 This is a sample letter we gave to all D-Team leaders at a meeting prior to camp. Along with this letter, leaders also received D-Team material to study and prepare.

Dear D-Team Leader:

After many weeks of prayer, preparation, and trying to get your students to turn in their registration forms, Impact University is almost here. As you think about the upcoming camp, you probably feel a sense of anticipation as well as nervousness. Take a deep breath and relax–you don't have to lead on your own. Relying on the Holy Spirit is the most important thing you can do as you lead your students during our time at camp.

At this camp, students will learn about our ministry's vision, mission, and strategy, as well as the role they can play in helping to build the ministry. The ministry season's theme, "Just For You," will be unveiled, and students will understand that the ministry really is "just for them." There will be an academic feel to this camp as students are "accepted" into the university upon registration and given diplomas at "graduation."

Take time to prepare yourself spiritually. Ask God how He could best use you and the gifts He has given you. Set aside time this week to listen to how God wants you to lead and shepherd the students He has entrusted to your care. Spend time praying for the students in your D-Team, asking God to draw them closer to Him. Also, pray that

- the students who have not yet accepted Christ will come to know Him at this camp.
- the students who are trying D-Teams out for the first time will have a positive experience.
- the students will understand our ministry's vision, mission, and strategy and desire to be committed core members.
- the message givers will communicate God's Word clearly and will be empowered by Him.
- there will be safety in travel.
- our ministry will receive protection.
- our leaders will have direction, discernment, and strength.

During Impact University, you will have the privilege of leading the students in your D-Team and helping them to become fully devoted followers of Christ. Your D-Team should sit together during mealtimes, the main sessions, and at the Concert of Prayer. Because you will be together during these sessions, you will have the opportunity to be creative and "own" your meeting area by decorating it or bringing notes or small gifts to your students each session. Keep the academic/collegiate theme in mind as you plan.

The D-Team material will give you all the information and ideas you will need to lead your D-Team throughout the week. There are also leadership meetings scheduled each day to keep you informed of the day's activities and also to answer any questions you may have. The following checklist will help you remember your main responsibilities for each session:

- Be prepared spiritually. Set aside time to pray and listen to God.
- Bring something to decorate your meeting area for each session.
  Possible ideas: personal notes, candy, gum, yearbooks, stuffed school mascots, pictures, etc. Be creative!
- Study the D-Team curriculum before you arrive at camp. You will find suggested questions and Scripture to use in each D-Team, so familiarize yourself with the material.
- Encourage students to be on time to all sessions and to bring their notebooks and Bibles. Lead by example.

Our time together is going to be incredible! Thank you for your commitment and passion to see high school students grow into fully devoted followers of Christ. Your role is so important and we greatly value and appreciate you. It will be exciting to serve together with you and to witness the amazing ways God is going to work through you to impact students' lives! Get ready–class is almost in session!

Camp Overview

Theme

The camp theme has an academic feel to it because students will be learning more about the student ministry and what part they can play in it. To get your students excited and enthusiastic about the university concept, tell them that those who are attending the camp have been "accepted" at the university and you want all campers to "graduate" with honors.

Handouts

Every student should be given some kind of handout or notebook to use for taking notes or journaling. You may want to include your retreat schedule in this handout as well as camp rules, a camp map, and information on various issues. Encourage students to bring their notebooks to all sessions and D-Teams.

Here are a few ideas for designing your student notebook:

- Develop written material and print into booklet form.
- Make stickers with the camp logo and stick them onto plain, inexpensive notebooks.
- Screen the camp logo onto 5 1/2" x 8 1/2" three-ring notebooks and build this expense into camp costs.

Take-Away

Consider giving each student some kind of tangible reminder of their camp experience. A take-away object plays an important part in reminding students of their time at camp and how God worked. Some possible ideas for a take-away for this camp include giving each student a diploma with his or her name on it signifying "graduation" from the university; a highlighter to remind them of their camp highlights; a pencil or pen with your ministry's name on it or the phrase, "Just For You"; a "yearbook" compiled after camp and filled with camp pictures and stories; or a graduation hat tassel.

Schedule

A sample daily schedule used by Student Impact for Impact University is included as a guideline to help you develop your own schedule. While schedules can be restrictive at times, they will keep your leaders and students organized each day and help make your time together purposeful.

Competition

Brainstorm with your leadership team a competitive activity that all your students will enjoy. It's fun to offer some kind of competition that requires scoring points so that you can announce a winning team.

Here are some suggestions for competition:

Cross Camp Race
This race involves completing stations set up all around the camp. The team that finishes all the stations first is the winner. Divide the group into two teams (or more if your group is large) and designate a captain for each team. For each station, the captain should determine who on his or her team will do each station. He or she should make sure that everyone has a chance to participate.

Before the Cross Camp Race begins, sing the National Anthem. To start the race, give one student from each team a

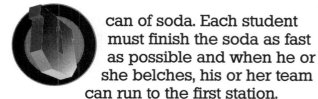 can of soda. Each student must finish the soda as fast as possible and when he or she belches, his or her team can run to the first station.

Possible stations could include:

Egg Toss–Two students from each team must toss the egg back and forth five times from a designated distance.

Horseshoes (if available)–A student must score 10 points before tagging the person to start the next station.

Volleyball Sets–Two students from each team must hit the volleyball over the net 15 consecutive times.

Bat Spin–A student must place his or her head on the top of a bat, spin around five times, and then jump over the bat (Watch out for this one!).

Ping-Pong Ball Roll–A student must blow a Ping-Pong ball on the ground a designated distance.

Saw the Log–A student must saw a log in half.

50-meter Swim (if available)–A student must swim 50 meters in a pool or lake.

Sourpuss–A student must eat one-half of a lemon.

Quarter-mile Run–A student must run a pre-set quarter mile around camp.

Mystery Station–A student must eat a mystery goulash dish prepared just for him or her (Let your imagination run wild!).

Water Balloon Toss–Two students from each team must toss a water balloon back and forth five times from a designated distance.

Canoe Race–Two students from each team must canoe a designated distance, turn around, and come back.

Volleyball
Set up a volleyball tournament with six students on a team. Have students name their team and make a tournament draw sheet on a piece of cardboard.

Search and Seizure
To play, divide into teams of 10–15 students per team and form a large circle. The competition leader stands in the middle of the circle and calls out different challenges for the teams to complete. For example, the competition leader might say, "**Build the largest human pyramid**"; "**Spell out [a certain word] using all your team members**"; "**Find three people on your team with a hole in their socks.**" Each completed challenge is awarded points based on the degree of difficulty. Determine your own point system based on your challenges. The team who scores the most points at the end of the camp wins.

Quiet Times

Throughout the week, give your students an opportunity to meet with God before breakfast for quiet times. For each morning of camp, you will find a suggested idea to share with your students. Encourage your leaders to use this time to assist any young believers who may be trying to do a quiet time for the first time. Keep in mind that these quiet times may encourage students to develop the spiritual discipline of reading the Bible and praying daily.

Ministry Activity

Take your entire group to a local attraction like a water park, a local sporting event, or a nearby city. Investigate what attractions are near your campsite and make arrangements before leaving for camp. Use this time to build community and a memory in your ministry and to have fun together.

D-Teams

D-Teams (small groups) give students a chance to discuss and apply what they are learning. The following descriptions give an overview of the D-Teams for the weekend:

D-Team #1–The Five Gs
Following the Saturday morning message, your D-Team will follow up on a personal level. You will help your students determine where they are with the five Gs and challenge them to move forward in areas they need to grow.

D-Team #2–Stay on the Mountain
During this D-Team session, you will answer the question **What is the purpose of community?** If there is a hill on the campgrounds, have your D-Team climb it together and then work through the questions. You will be brainstorming how to stay walking with Christ throughout the year.

D-Team #3–Next Year: Just For You
In this D-Team session, you will be answering the question **If this student ministry is just for me, then what do I need it to be in order for me to grow in Christ?**

Programs

All programming elements are designed to move each student emotionally and intellectually to see God's love by exposing God's truth in a relevant, practical way through the communicative arts. Each program points students toward a basic biblical truth. Sample Cue Sheets include suggested program orders.

Here are a few ideas, materials, and props you may want to use in planning your programs:

Ideas
1. Hold your planning sessions with your team on a local college campus. Sit in the cafeteria or snack shop and make observations about college life. Find out what the latest crazes are and what is current on the college campus.
2. Dust off your college yearbook and flip through it for creative sparks. You could probably have some fun with your class picture–or maybe not!
3. Visit with a college professor to feel the "aura" of academia.
4. Watch movies with classroom or collegiate scenes, such as *Dead Poets' Society, Ferris Buehler's Day Off,* or *Rudy.* If you find any scenes that would be appropriate for your students, play them during the programs or show the whole movie for a possible evening activity.
5. Organize the chairs in your meeting area "lecture-style." Make the area look and feel like a college classroom.

Materials/Props
You can creatively use props in your programs to further develop the theme visually. To make the program area look collegiate, place gothic/Roman columns and a chalkboard up front. You may want to give a scholarly feel by going "Greek" and having your leaders wear sandals and togas–kind of a Socrates/Plato look!

Messages

The four messages included in this camp are geared to teach vision, mission, strategy, and any other key values that drive your ministry. Try to make all of your teaching times interactive and creative. Use the material provided, but take time to hear what the Holy Spirit wants to communicate to your students through you.

Here are brief summaries of the evening and morning messages:

Friday Evening Message–Youth Group vs. Student Ministry
In this message, students will learn the differences between a youth group and a student ministry.

Saturday Morning Message–Fully Devoted Followers
Students will be challenged to become

fully devoted followers of Jesus Christ by looking at five areas in their lives.

Saturday Evening Message–Building Community
In this message, students will learn about the power of community that can be found in D-Teams.

Sunday Evening Message–Just For You
This message will let students know that your student ministry is committed to meeting their needs and that it can be a place "Just For You."

Team Builders

Building a sense of team among students is critical. The suggested Team Builder exercises will be most effective if students are placed on campus teams according to the high school they attend. These exercises will create an atmosphere where your students can interact on a deeper spiritual level with other students on their campus team and also with the members of their D-Team. Team building will challenge, teach, and encourage your students.

These exercises also provide your leaders an opportunity to further build relationships with students. There are three scheduled times for teams to meet during camp, and they vary in length. For instance, the second Team Builder includes only a few questions to be discussed because it follows a D-Team and a message. The third Team Builder is flexible and agenda-free to allow you and your leaders to cast a vision for your particular team. You will need to plan for that time.

Here is a brief overview of each Team Builder exercise:

Team Builder #1–Who Are We?
This first Team Builder follows the message time and takes a closer look at what was just taught. The question to be answered during the team builder time is: **Is our team more like a youth group or a student ministry?** During the message, your campus team will break into D-Teams, take a test, and discuss the results.

Team Builder #2–Empty Chair
During this Team Builder, you will evaluate your D-Teams and the use of the empty chair within each one of them. This will give you a good reading on your core students and their evangelistic efforts.

Team Builder #3–Team Vision
In this Team Builder, you and the leaders on your team will have a chance to communicate the "Just For You" vision for your team and what that really means for your particular team for the rest of the ministry season. Each team will have a unique way to carry out this vision. Therefore, the agenda needs to be determined by each team's leaders.

FRIDAY

Schedule

4:00 PM	Registration	9:30 PM	Evening Session– **Youth Group vs. Student Ministry**
5:00 PM	Buses Leave		
7:45 PM	Arrive at Camp	11:00 PM	Team Builder #1– **Who Are We?**
8:00 PM	Impact University Orientation	12:30 PM	Lights Out
8:30 PM	Room Check-in		

Impact University Orientation Program Cue Sheet

TIME	PROGRAM ELEMENT

8:00 PM   DOORS OPEN/WALK-IN
Play *Pomp & Circumstance* via an audiotape.

8:05 PM   WELCOME
Host welcomes students and lets them know they have been accepted into the university.

8:10 PM   SONG
Select an "up-tempo" contemporary Christian song to kick off the camp.

8:14 PM   INTRODUCTION OF CAMP THEME AND SCHEDULE
Host briefly explains the camp theme and reviews the camp schedule.

8:19 PM   UNIVERSITY RULES
Host states the camp rules, like the three Ms:
1. Be at all **m**eals.
2. Be at all **m**eetings.
3. Be **m**odest in all you do and say.
You could communicate the rules in a creative way, using a Top 10 List, like "The Top 10 Ways to Get Kicked Out of the University." For example, #10–Get drunk; #9–Skip sessions; #8–Sleep in a member of the opposite sex's room, etc.

8:29 PM   DISMISS TO CHECK-IN
Host gives instructions for check-in and then dismisses.

Friday
Evening Session

Program Cue Sheet

TIME	PROGRAM ELEMENT

TIME   **PROGRAM ELEMENT**

9:30 PM   **DOORS OPEN/WALK-IN**
Play some "high-energy" Christian music.

9:35 PM   **WELCOME**
Host welcomes everyone to the university and shares a personal experience from his or her college days as an icebreaker.

9:37 PM   **WORSHIP**
Worship leader selects five to seven worship choruses. (See Appendix C for a list of choruses.)

9:57 PM   **TESTIMONIES**
You or a leader should sit with two students up front and "interview" them about their experience in your student ministry. Ask them how their lives have changed because of Christ and how the ministry has helped them to keep growing spiritually. Carefully select students before this session and prepare them on the kinds of questions you will be asking them. Use these testimonies to lead into your message time.

10:05 PM   **MESSAGE–YOUTH GROUP VS. STUDENT MINISTRY**
See Friday Evening Message rationale and outline.

10:35 PM   **ANNOUNCEMENTS AND DISMISS**
Host should pray, give the schedule for the next day, and dismiss students to their Team Builder time.

Friday Evening Message–
Youth Group vs. Student Ministry

Big Idea

When most people hear the term *youth group,* they usually think of youth in church. Many high school departments in the church today tend to be small groups of students who lack a vision for their non-Christian friends and fail to look outside their inner circle. A *student ministry,* on the other hand, is a group of students who actively participate in carrying out the ministry's vision on their campus and have compassion for their non-Christian friends. They have experienced life change and they want their friends to as well.

Rationale

Every one of us can begin to help transform a youth group into an effective student ministry by looking at the differences between the two.

Message Outline

I. Characteristics of a Youth Group
   a. Is activity-driven.
      • The calendar is the prevailing force.
      • Activities become the sole reason for gathering.
   b. Sticks with traditions and forgets to ask the question "Why?"
      • Often does things because that is the way it has always been done.
   c. Lacks vision and direction.
      • Without vision, which brings purpose, students and leaders burn out or are confused about where the ministry is headed.
   d. Students have a tendency to focus inward which can lead to stagnation and minimum growth.
      • With little or no evangelism focus, students become comfortable and casual with their Christian "cliques."
      • Compassion for non-Christians is often missing.
      • There is no ownership or accountability for sharing Christ.

II. Characteristics of a Student Ministry
   a. Is purpose-driven.
      • Students know that every activity has a purpose.
      • Students aren't afraid to ask "Why?" and "Is it working?"

Friday Evening Message–(cont.)
Youth Group vs. Student Ministry

b. Communicates the vision regularly.
  • It is the leader's responsibility to share the vision (*where*), mission (*why*), and strategy (*how*) of the ministry.
  • Students become players instead of spectators.
  • Students understand their role in the bigger ministry picture.
  • Being young does not exclude students from being God's ambassadors (1 Timothy 4:12).

c. Students have compassion for non-Christians and are excited about evangelism.
  • Matthew 28:19–students' focus is outward, not inward.
  • Students see God working in their own lives and want to share that work.

d. Values prayer and worship.
  • Students focus on the Lord in worship and spend time in individual and corporate prayer.

e. Provides accountability and acceptance.
  • In small groups, students can find safety, value, and a place to be heard.
  • Students can sharpen each other in peer groups led by mature leaders.

III. Evaluating Our Ministry
  a. Ask the hard questions to students.
    • Are you becoming more like Christ?
    • Do you have compassion for your non-Christian friends?
    • Do you know your ministry's vision, mission, and strategy?
    • Do you regularly participate in corporate worship and prayer as well as individual prayer?
    • Are there friends in your life who hold you accountable?
  b. Ask the hard questions to leaders.
    • Is the ministry vision fresh in your mind and soul, or is it lost due to tasks of "doing ministry"?
    • Has God filled your heart with passion for student ministry?
    • Are you using your top spiritual gift in the position you currently serve in or do adjustments need to be made?
  c. The Youth Group vs. Student Ministry Test (Distribute copies of **Student Notes** #1 to students– What Kind of Ministry?)
    • Allows for honest evaluation of your group.
    • Give directions on how to take this test during Team Builder #1.

Team Builder # 1 –
Who Are We?

Preparation

To prepare for this Team Builder, you need to select four students ahead of time to help you carry out the opening exercise. Inform two volunteers to lie down on the sheet as soon as you put it on the ground. Instruct your other two volunteers to walk over to the sheet and try to pick it up. Tell them they are not to ask other students for help, but they can let others join in if they want to help. If other students ask what they are doing, they can tell them that they were asked to carry the two volunteers from the original spot to 100 feet away. Following the exercise, break your students into D-Teams (small groups) to work through the **What Kind of Ministry?** test referred to during Message #1.

Materials Needed

- One old sheet–preferably king-size
- Copies of Student Notes #1 and #2

Exercise

To begin the exercise, place a sheet on the floor. Your first two volunteers should lie down on the sheet. Don't explain to your students what is expected of them. Give your students approximately 10 minutes to complete the given project and then call them together.

Note: *If the whole team gets involved, join them as a participant. Don't be left standing there observing!*

Follow-up

Your students may respond to the exercise in several ways:
- The whole group may participate right away.
- Some students may take a little while

to work together to complete the project.
- Some students may never catch on to what is happening and the two guys may lie there for 10 minutes.

Have your students sit in a circle so that they can look at each other. Then discuss the following questions:
- What caused you to participate in this exercise if no one told you what to do?
- Did you think that the students carrying the sheet needed help?
- Did you want to be involved in what was going on?
- What do you think about the group's response to what was happening?
- Are you happy with how you responded? Why or why not?
- Do you think we worked together as a team?
- What if the students on the sheet were dying–how would your response have been different? Why?

Explain that everyone will be breaking into D-Teams to take the **What Kind of Ministry?** test referred to during Message #1. Ask your students to be honest with their answers. Distribute copies of Student Notes #1, dismiss your students to meet for 15–20 minutes, and then ask them to come back and share their responses to the test.

Close this Team Builder by having a couple of students pray for the D-Team meetings and the effect they will have on the student ministry during the coming year. Then distribute copies of Student Notes #2 and encourage your students to spend some time with God in the morning.

Saturday

Schedule

7:00 AM   Quiet Time

8:00 AM   Breakfast

9:00 AM   Morning Session–
Fully Devoted Followers

10:00 AM   D-Team #1–
The Five Gs

11:00 AM   Competition

12:30 PM   Lunch

1:30 PM   Leaders' Meeting

1:30 PM   Free Time

5:00 PM   Dinner

6:00 PM   One-on-Ones

7:00 PM   D-Team #2–
Stay on the Mountain

8:30 PM   Evening Session–
Building Community

10:00 PM   Team Builder #2–
Empty Chair

12:30 AM   Lights Out

Saturday Morning Session Program Cue Sheet

TIME	PROGRAM ELEMENT
9:00 AM	**DOORS OPEN/WALK-IN** Play some "high-energy" Christian music.
9:03 AM	**WORSHIP** Worship leader selects three worship choruses.
9:15 AM	**MESSAGE– FULLY DEVOTED FOLLOWERS** See Saturday Morning Message rationale and outline.
9:45 AM	**SONG** Have a vocalist sing, or play a CD of a song about spiritual growth.
9:50 AM	**ANNOUNCEMENTS AND DISMISS** Host prays and dismisses students to their D-Teams.

Saturday Morning Message–Fully Devoted Followers

Big Idea

Many people have no idea of what a real Christian looks like. Students feel that same tension as they attempt to become *committed* Christians. In this session, we will look at the five areas that characterize a committed Christian (or what we refer to as a fully devoted follower).

Rationale

Every person can fulfill the mission of the student ministry by becoming a fully devoted follower of Jesus Christ by examining and developing his or her life in five areas:

- Grace
- Growth
- Group
- Gifts
- Giving

Message Outline

I. The Mission of a Student Ministry
   a. Student Impact's mission: To reach unbelieving high school students and help them become fully devoted followers of Jesus Christ.
   b. Your student ministry: Define your mission.
      - Should include both evangelism and discipleship.
      - Should include a challenge for student growth.

II. The Characteristics of a Fully Devoted Follower
   a. Grace.
      - Why we need grace: Romans 3:10–18; Galatians 3:22.
      - What God offers: Matthew 11:28–30; Isaiah 1:18; 1 John 1:8–9; Romans 8:1.
      - Why we do not have to or cannot earn God's acceptance: Ephesians 2:8–9; Titus 3:4–7.
      - How God handles the debt of our sin: 1 Peter 2:24; Hebrews 10:10–14.
      - What to do when we are ready for God's help and forgiveness: John 1:11–12; Acts 16:30–31; Romans 10:9; Galatians 2:16.
      - A common response of new believers to grace: Acts 2:37–38, 41; 8:36–38; 16:14–15.
   b. Growth.
      - Characteristics of believers: Ephesians 4:14–15; 2 Peter 3:17–18.
      - Tools for growth.
      - The Bible: Psalm 1:2–3; Hebrews 4:12; Psalm 119:9–24.

- Prayer/Solitude/Worship:
  Luke 5:16; 6:12–13;
  Ephesians 6:18; Psalm 145:1–7.
- Spiritual disciplines:
  Ephesians 3:16–19.

c. Group.
  - Why community was valued by the early church: Acts 2:44–47; 4:32–35; Hebrews 10:24–25.
  - Small group examples in the Bible: Mark 3:14; Acts 2:46; 1 Corinthians 16:19.

d. Gifts.
  - What spiritual gifts are: 1 Corinthians 12:14–26.
  - Why they differ in different people: 1 Corinthians 12:4–7.
  - What the source of differences is: Romans 12:4–8.
  - What is our responsibility: 1 Corinthians 15:58.

e. Good stewardship.
  - What the Bible says about giving: Genesis 14:18–20; Leviticus 27:30, 32; Malachi 3:8–10.
  - What the Bible says about ownership: Luke 14:33; 16:10–13.
  - What the Bible says about savings and debt: Proverbs 6:6–11; 28:20; 21:25–26; 22:7, 26–27.
  - What the Bible says about attitude toward money and giving: 1 Timothy 6:8–10, 17–19; 1 Corinthians 16:1–2; 2 Corinthians 8:9, 12; 9:6–9; Luke 6:38; Matthew 6:3–4.

III. How Can You Identify a Fully Devoted Follower?
  a. A student who personally understands the grace of God and has trusted Him as Savior.
  b. A student who has committed to spiritual growth and demonstrates a pattern of life change.
  c. A student who is committed to a small group of fellow believers to pursue maturity and community.
  d. A student who is learning to express his or her God-given gifts as a servant of Christ.
  e. A student who is participating in God's work in the church through good stewardship of his or her resources.

IV. Challenge to Students
  a. What "G" of the fully devoted mission do you need to develop?
  b. Who will you tell for accountability?

D-Team #1 –
The Five Gs

Objective

The goal of this D-Team experience is to follow up on a personal level on what was just taught: the five Gs. You will help your students determine where they are at with each of the five Gs and challenge them to take steps of growth where needed. Be sure to study the five Gs on your own so that you are prepared to answer your students' questions. We have seen students come to know Christ after learning about the first G–Grace.

Materials Needed

- Bibles
- Copies of Student Notes #3

The Five Gs

Read each description aloud before asking the questions that follow.

Grace (Ephesians 2:8–9)
Followers of Christ understand and have individually received His saving grace. They have abandoned all attempts to earn God's favor through accomplishments of their own, and they find security only through Christ's sacrificial death on their behalf. In obedience to Christ's command, they have undergone water baptism as believers, giving outward witness to the inner cleansing and renewal experienced in Him.

Growth (2 Peter 3:18)
Followers of Christ know that the saving grace of God is only the beginning of His work in them. They gratefully respond by actively pursuing a lifelong process of spiritual growth in Christ and seek to become conformed to His image. To this end, they consistently nurture their spiritual development through prayer, worship, and Bible study. They regard the Bible as the final authority in all areas about which it teaches, and desire to be wholly obedient to it. Followers of Christ honestly confront areas of personal sin and engage the Holy Spirit's power in seeking to turn from sin. They also desire to extend the grace they've received to others through personal evangelism and participation in the collective ministry of the church in their community, their country, and around the world.

Group (Acts 2:46)
A follower of Christ honors God's call to participate in community in order to grow in Christlikeness, express and receive love, and carry out the ministry of the church. For this reason, followers of Christ give priority to attending the corporate gatherings of the church for the purpose of worship, teaching, and participation in the sacrament of communion, and are connected relationally to a small group of believers for the purpose of mutual encouragement, support, and accountability. Followers of Christ also pursue Christ-honoring relationships wherever they are, support the leadership of the church and are biblically submissive to it, and affirm and uphold the fundamental truths of Scripture.

Gifts (Romans 12:6–8)
Followers of Christ recognize that the church is composed of interdependent members, each uniquely gifted by the Holy Spirit for the purpose of building up the body and furthering the ministry of the church. Therefore, they seek to discover, develop, and deploy those God-given gifts and to look for a place of service within the church, with the support and affirmation of the body.

Good Stewardship (Philippians 4:11–19)
Followers of Christ realize that they have been bought with the price of Christ's blood, and that everything they are and have belongs to Him. In light of this, they desire to be responsible caretakers of the material resources that God has entrusted to them. They recognize the tithe (10 percent of one's earnings) as the historic standard of giving in Scripture. But, moreover, in response to Christ's abundant giving, they increasingly submit their resources to His lordship and display a spirit of generosity and cheerfulness in supporting the work of the church.

Distribute copies of Student Notes #3 and have your students answer the following questions to determine where they are with the five Gs. After completing these questions, determine where each person needs encouragement in his or her life. Then affirm your students with what they have done and what they need to work on. Be sure to follow up with each student individually after this D-Team. Take notes on each student's response.

Grace

- Have you ever accepted God's grace into your life? When and where?
- What does your grace gauge look like? Do you accept God's grace daily in your life? Do you extend that grace to other people around you? Why or why not?
- Maybe this is the "G" that you need to work through in your life. Ask your D-Team members to support you in this area of your life.

Growth

- Prayer, worship, and Bible study are vital elements in deepening one's walk with Christ. Are you nurturing your spiritual growth on your own through those spiritual disciplines? How often and what are you doing?

Note: *In asking your students to describe their spiritual habits, be careful to avoid the mistaken notion that legalistic formulas and rigid rules guarantee a healthy devotional life. It is more important that their walk with Christ simply be characterized by regular and meaningful* *input. What matters is that they're becoming more like Him and that they're taking it on themselves to improve their relationship with Him privately, not depending solely on what public meetings provide.*

- In your pursuit of becoming more Christlike, what areas are most difficult for you?
- What does your growth gauge look like? Do you see it as being low or high at this point in your life?
- Maybe this is the "G" that you need to work through in your life. Ask your D-Team members to support you in this area of your life.

Group

- Do you regularly participate in the corporate gatherings of your ministry? Why or why not?
- Are you connected to a small group of believers for the purpose of growth, loving support, and accountability? Why or why not? How is your group doing?
- What does your group gauge look like? Do you see it as balanced in this area or do you need to make some changes?
- Maybe this is the "G" that you need to work through in your life. Ask your D-Team members to support you in this area of your life.

Gifts

- Are you interested in finding out what spiritual gifts God has given you to use in a place of service within the church?
- Are you currently finding out what your gifts are?
- If you already know what your spiritual gifts are, are you presently using them in an area of service within your youth ministry? Within another ministry at your church? If not, why not?
- What does your gifts gauge look like? Do you feel as though you are pursuing your gifts to the best of your ability?
- Maybe this is the "G" that you need to work through in your life. Ask your D-Team members to support you in this area of your life.

Good Stewardship

- Do you regularly support this youth ministry using 10 percent as a goal to reach?
- What does your stewardship gauge look like? Do you see it resting in the healthy range in your life right now?
- Maybe this is the "G" that you need to work through in your life. Ask your D-Team members to support you in this area of your life.

In Closing

This opportunity to take a spiritual inventory should be rich and affirming. Remember, you are not looking for "perfect Christians" who live struggle-free lives. You are looking for those who are committed to Christ, to His church, and to ongoing growth. Pray for each D-Team member by putting him or her in the middle of the circle and praying for the area that he or she really wants to focus on in life.

Saturday Morning Competition–
Cross Camp Race

This race involves completing stations set up all around the camp. The team that finishes all the stations first is the winner. Divide the group into two teams (or more if your group is large) and designate a captain for each team. For each station, the captain should determine who on his or her team will do each station. He or she should make sure that everyone has a chance to participate.

Before the Cross Camp Race begins, sing your country's national anthem. To start the race, give one student from each team a can of soda. Each student must finish the soda as fast as possible and when he or she belches, his or her team can run to the first station.

Possible stations could include

Egg Toss–Two students from each team must toss the egg back and forth five times from a designated distance.

Horseshoes (if available)–A student must score 10 points before tagging the person to start the next station.

Volleyball Sets–Two students from each team must hit the volleyball over the net 15 consecutive times.

Bat Spin–A student must place his or her head on the top of a bat, spin around five times, and then jump over the bat (Watch out for this one!).

Ping-Pong Ball Roll–A student must blow a Ping-Pong ball on the ground a designated distance.

Saw the Log–A student must saw a log in half.

50-meter Swim (if available)–A student must swim 50 meters in a pool or lake.

Sourpuss–A student must eat one-half of a lemon.

Quarter-mile Run–A student must run a pre-set quarter mile around camp.

Mystery Station–A student must eat a mystery goulash dish prepared just for him or her (Let your imagination run wild!).

Water Balloon Toss–Two students from each team must toss a water balloon back and forth five times from a designated distance.

Canoe Race–Two students from each team must canoe a designated distance, turn around, and come back.

Optional Competition–Volleyball

Set up a volleyball tournament with six students on a team. Have students name their team and make a tournament draw sheet on a piece of cardboard.

Optional Competition–
Search and Seizure

To play, divide into teams of 10-15 students per team and form a large circle. The competition leader stands in the middle of the circle and calls out different challenges for the teams to complete. For example, the competition leader might say, **"Build the largest human pyramid"; "Spell out [a certain word] using all your team members"; "Find three people on your team with a hole in their socks."** Each completed challenge is awarded points based on the degree of difficulty. Determine your own point system based on your challenges. The team who scores the most points at the end of the camp wins.

D-Team #2–
Stay on the Mountain

Objective

During this experience, your students will answer the question **What is the purpose of community?** Although Christian community takes many forms, you will focus on your D-Team, comparing your D-Team to a mountain as a safe place to gain perspective on our relationship with God and others. Every D-Team member will discover that Christian community gives us two perspectives:

- Perspective on Ourselves
- Perspective on Others

Materials Needed

- Bibles
- Recording of Steven Curtis Chapman's "The Mountain" (*Heaven in the Real World*, Sparrow, 1994)
- Tape/CD player
- A watch

Climbing a Hill

Take your students to the bottom of a hill. Instruct them to spread at least arm's-length apart from each other, facing the hill. Ask them to close their eyes and stand quietly for the next three minutes. Join your D-Team members in this experience, but keep track of the time. After the three minutes are over, ask your students to open their eyes and link arms to walk up the hill together. Find a place at the top of the hill to meet together.

Gather your students in a circle and discuss these questions: **How did you feel standing at the bottom of the hill? Alone? Afraid that everyone had left you? Unsure? What did you think about? How did you feel when you were able to open your eyes? How does sitting in this circle feel different than being at the bottom of the hill with your eyes closed? Which place would you rather be right now?**

Perspective on Ourselves

Explain to your students that today they will discover the purpose of a D-Team. Ask them to think of being part of a D-Team as like climbing a mountain. We can experience God wherever we are, but going up on a mountain allows our experience to be a safe place away from the dark valley we live in.

Ask your students to list the possible purposes of a D-Team. Their answers may include: friendships, prayer for each other, studying God's Word.

Have students look up the following passages to discover three essentials for building closer relationships with Christ and His body.

Psalm 100 (Worship the Lord together.)
Psalm 119:9–16 and 2 Timothy 3:16 (Study the Word together.)
James 5:16 (Prayer and accountability.)

Discuss how your D-Team can build closer relationships with Christ and with one another through these three essentials.

Perspective on Others

Ask, **"What other perspective can we gain from being on the mountain? We have looked inward; what else can we look at from up here?"** Note that being on the mountain gives us a clearer perspective on those who are still alone down in the valley.

D-Team #2–
Stay on the Mountain

Ask your D-Team to stay in a circle, but turn around and face outward. Have your students leave an open space in the circle to represent an empty chair for another new person who may come up the mountain. Ask them to describe what they can see now that they couldn't see from the bottom of the hill.

Then take a moment to remember: **How did you feel when you were at the bottom of the hill? Alone? Unsure? No one to lean on?** Emphasize that there are still people down there . . . alone. Friends, family, neighbors, and classmates.

Explain that the other purpose of a D-Team is evangelism. Your students will not be able to ignore the people in the valley; they will want to bring those lonely, distraught people up to experience the mountain with them. Remind your students that they don't have to do it alone–they have their fellow D-Team members to assist them.

Say, **"Steven Curtis Chapman wrote a song that describes what we talked about today."** Read the lyrics to your D-Team members and then listen to the song "The Mountain." Close in prayer, asking God to help you and your D-Team members see a new, clearer picture of the full purpose of D-Teams.

In Closing

Have your students walk down the hill together and stand alone again for three minutes. Challenge each student to picture a friend standing in the valley alone, waiting for a guide up the mountain. Ask, **"What is the person's name?"** Urge students to pray for these unsaved friends. Allow your students to decide if they want to choose one person to pray for as a group, or if each wants to pray for a different friend.

Saturday
Evening Session

Program Cue Sheet

TIME	PROGRAM ELEMENT

8:30 PM   **DOORS OPEN/WALK-IN**
Select some "high-energy" Christian music.

8:35 PM   **WORSHIP**
Worship leader selects five to seven worship choruses.

8:55 PM   **SCRIPTURE READING**
Ask a student or leader to read a passage about God's heart for lost people, such as Luke 5:30–32; Luke 15; or Matthew 18:14.

9:00 PM   **DRAMA–GO FISH**
This drama focuses on evangelism and should be rehearsed before camp and at least once during camp. Use students who have an ability to act and would enjoy participating in this way.

9:06 PM   **MESSAGE– BUILDING COMMUNITY**
See Saturday Evening Message rationale and outline.

9:36 PM   **SONG AND VIDEO**
Have a vocalist sing, or play a CD of DC Talk's "I Wish We'd All Been Ready" from (*Jesus Freak,* ForeFront, 1995) while a video of your students is shown in the background.

9:41 PM   **WORSHIP**
Worship leader chooses choruses focused on our responsibility to share Christ with lost people.

10:00 PM   **ANNOUNCEMENTS AND DISMISS**
Host prays and dismisses students to their Team Builder time.

Drama Script–Go Fish

Scene is four students in a rowboat on a small lake on the grounds of Disney World. All four have fishing poles. Molly and Jeff have their poles in the water. Molly has caught three fish already, Jeff none. Julie tries unsuccessfully to bait her pole, and Pete sits with pole at his side, unwilling to join in and nervous about the whole adventure. Scene opens where they are in the middle of singing the Noah's Ark song:

Molly, Jeff, Julie: (singing) The animals they came on, they came on by threezies threezies, the animals they came on by threezies, threezies, elephants and chimpanzeezies zeezies, children of ...

Pete: (has been trying to quiet them for a while) Shhh! Quiet you guys!

Julie: What?

Pete: I thought I heard something.

Julie: Well, there are about 3 billion people over at Disney World right now. . . .

Molly: And about 20 billion bugs, fish, reptiles, birds, and other living creatures surrounding us ...

Julie: (holding up can in disgust) Not to mention the worms that are with us!

Pete: No, I heard a person ... like a cop or something.

Jeff: C'mon Pete, lighten up! We're on vacation!

Pete: We're not supposed to be on vacation here.

Jeff: Hey ... we're supposed to be at Disney World ... this pond is part of Disney World.

Julie: Besides, what better group of people to get in trouble with than your best buds?

Molly: (pole jerking) Oh! I got another one!

Jeff: How do you do that? Let's switch places. The point must be the lucky spot. (they do, rather clumsily)

Molly: Watch the line!

Julie: Oh, I almost had a potato chip on my hook and you bumped it!

Jeff: You're using chips for bait ?

Molly: She just doesn't want to touch the worms! Pass 'em over, will ya?

Julie: I'll get one of these to stay on yet! (cracks another chip on hook)

Pete: Pipe down, will ya?

Jeff: Have a chip, Pete. (passes the bag to him)

Molly: Come on Pete, we all thought it would be fun to take out a boat on our last night here ... (looks up)

Pete: I just don't want to get in trouble.

Molly: (looking up) ... and what a great night.

Julie: (looking up) Awesome! Look at all those stars. (everyone looking up, gets a bit introspective here ... even Pete ... lots of pauses)

Molly: (pause) Did you ever wonder why God decided stars? I mean, why not, illuminated floating zebras or something?

Jeff: What?

Molly: Well, God could do it if He wanted.

Jeff: Yeah, I suppose.

Julie: I'm glad He chose stars.

Molly: Why?

Julie: Because zebras poop. (does motion of something falling from the sky and landing on her lap) (others laugh)

Molly: (pause) I don't want to go home.

Julie: Me either ... I just want to hang out with you guys for the rest of the summer.

Pete: Yeah, me too . . . but not in jail.

Molly: (pole shakes) I got another one!

Julie: Oh man! I still can't get a chip on my hook! (tries again)

Jeff: (has been listening to this and gets an idea ... stands up fast and dramatically says) I get it!

Julie: Get what?

Pete: Get down!

Rick: (offstage voice) Ahoy Mates! (everyone ducks down in boat)

Julie: (whispers) Who is it?

Molly: (whispers) I don't know!

Pete: (whispers) We're gonna die!

Rick: Hey! It's me, Rick Chambers!

Jim: (pause, everyone is still down, whispers) Who's Rick Chambers?

Molly: (whispers) Isn't he that guy from the church in Michigan?

Jim: Oh yeah! (gets up) Hey, Rick! (the girls get up and wave)

Pete: Shhh! It might be a trick!

Rick: (yelling) Got room for one more out there?

All except Pete: Yeah!

Pete: No! (in unison ... they look at him)

Molly: Why not?

Pete: Because he's not in our group ... he might snitch on us or something.

Julie: Maybe Pete is right.

Molly: But he's already seen us! Besides, I think it would be fun! The more the merrier!

Jim: This is so awesome.

Julie: Jim, quit looking at the scenery. We need to make a decision here.

Jim: I know, what an awesome analogy ... of Jesus and His disciples.

Pete: Disney World?

Julie: Worms?

Jim: No, I mean when Christ said He'd make them fishers of men ... I never really understood the full meaning of that ... until now. I mean, look at us, Molly there is catching fish left and right ... she's into it, she's got the equipment and she's using it. Just like us ... with evangelism. We've been taught tons this week ... our equipment, now we just gotta, well, go fishing. And Julie ... you're so worried about the worms and getting the bait on the hook, that you've missed all the fish.

Julie: (getting it) How many people have I "missed" because I didn't think I was ready to tell them about Christ?

Jim: Exactly! And Pete here is just so worried about doing the wrong thing ... well, that he's missing the right thing.

Rick: HEL-LO! What do you guys say! Are you coming to get me or not?

Jim: We can't just stay in our little group ... we gotta "go fish," you guys.

Molly: He's right.

Julie: Give me the worms!

Pete: Give me the oars!

Jim: Full steam ahead!

Saturday Evening Message–
Building Community

Big Idea
Life change happens best in small relational groups of like-minded believers. D-Teams ("D" for the Greek *delta,* which means change) are groups of students committed to God and each other, who desire their lives to be changed by becoming more devoted to Jesus Christ. D-Teams build community and should be a vital part of every Christian's life.

Rationale
We can understand the value of D-Teams by looking at three key truths found in the book of Acts:
- Devotion to one another
- Value of each person
- Commitment to community within the body of Christ

Message Outline
I. Community in the Early Church
    Read Acts 2:42–47 to paint the picture of the early church and their commitment to one another. What can we learn from this passage?
    a. They were devoted to one another (2:42).
        - They had a "hands in the middle" kind of attitude.
        - We too should help one another (see also Galatians 6:1–3).
        - We can sharpen one another to grow spiritually (Proverbs 27:17).
    b. Each person was a valuable part of the community (Acts 2:44).
        - They met each other's needs.
        - We each have been given a spiritual gift to contribute to the body (1 Corinthians 12:4–7).
        - We can teach each other (Colossians 3:16).
    c. They were committed to community within the body of Christ (Acts 2:46).
        - They worshiped together.
        - They committed to meeting together (see also Hebrews 10:24–25).
        - They added people to their community (Acts 2:47).

II. Community in Your D-Team
    a. How can you be devoted to the members of your D-Team?
    b. Do you value each person in your D-Team?
    c. Are you committed to community? Explain the "empty" chair concept: All D-Teams need to be open, not closed, so that others can fill the "empty" chair and experience community in their D-Team.

Team Builder #2–
Empty Chair

Preparation
During this Team Builder, you will evaluate your D-Teams and the use of the empty chair within each. This should give you an overall reading on how your students are doing with filling the empty chair. Keep in mind that this Team Builder is scheduled at the end of a full day when your students will most likely be tired. You need to have a high energy level as you lead your students.

Materials Needed
- Copies of Student Notes #4

Evaluation
Ask your students to sit with their D-Teams as they discuss the following questions:
- Did you ever sit in the empty chair? How did you feel? How did it affect your life?
- Did you use the empty chair as a D-Team? When and with whom?
- What keeps you from using the empty chair? (fear of rejection; fear of reputation getting ruined; just don't care; never thought twice about it; don't want outsiders to come in)
- Will you commit, as a D-Team member, to praying for a friend to fill the empty chair in your D-Team?

In Closing
Close in prayer for friends to fill the empty chairs in your D-Teams. Distribute copies of Student Notes #4–Sunday Morning Quiet Time.

Sunday

Schedule

7:00 AM Quiet Time

8:00 AM Breakfast

8:30 AM Leaders' Meeting

9:00 AM Buses Leave for Off-Site
Activity

10:30 AM Ministry Activity

12:00 PM Lunch

4:30 PM Buses Return to Campsite

6:00 PM Dinner

7:00 PM One-on-Ones

8:00 PM Evening Session–
Just For You

9:00 PM D-Team #3–
Next Year: Just For You

10:30 PM Concert of Prayer

Ministry Activity

Take your entire group to a local attraction like a water park, a local sporting event, or a nearby city. Investigate what attractions are near your campsite and make arrangements before leaving for camp. Use this time to build community and a memory in your ministry and to have fun together.

Sunday Evening Session Program Cue Sheet

TIME	PROGRAM ELEMENT
8:00 PM	**DOORS OPEN/WALK-IN** Select some "high-energy" Christian music.
8:03 PM	**INTRODUCTION** Host opens the session in prayer and introduces the evening's topic.
8:06 PM	**SONG** Have a vocalist sing, or play a CD of a song focused on growing in Christ.
8:10 PM	**MESSAGE–JUST FOR YOU** See Sunday Evening Message rationale and outline.
8:40 PM	**WORSHIP** Worship leader selects five to seven worship choruses which are more reflective and mid-tempo to prepare students for the Concert of Prayer later this evening.
8:55 PM	**ANNOUNCEMENTS AND DISMISS** Host prays and dismisses students to their D-Teams.

Sunday Evening Message–
Just For You

Big Idea

Students want to be led and need to know exactly where they are being led. In this message, students will hear your ministry's vision and clearly understand where the ministry is headed for the rest of the season. They will hear that the ministry is "Just For You."

Rationale

Every one of us can learn about the power of vision by knowing three things:
- What vision is.
- Why vision needs to be shared.
- Where our ministry is headed.

Message Outline

I. What Is Vision?
   a. "Vision for ministry is a reflection of what God wants to accomplish through you to build His kingdom. . . . Vision is not dreaming the impossible dream, but dreaming the most possible dream" (George Barna, *The Power of Vision*, Regal, 1992, p. 30). Vision is essential for kingdom building.
   b. Vision answers the question: Where is the ministry going?
   c. Vision provides an attractive and exciting future for a group of people.
   d. Vision creates a noble cause.

II. Why Vision Needs to Be Shared
   a. People (students) want and need a cause; they want to follow.
   b. Read Proverbs 29:18. Vision breathes life into people.
   c. Without it, stagnation and boredom can set in.

III. Our Ministry Vision
   a. Student Impact's Vision: a unique community of students and leaders committed to letting God change their lives, change their friends' lives, build the church, and impact the world.
      • This year's vision will focus on the theme "Just For You." This ministry can be "Just For You" and help you grow in your walk with Christ.
   b. Communicate your ministry's unique vision.
      • Should include both evangelism and discipleship.
      • Should be a reflection of your heart and what God is telling you.
      • Should reflect the uniqueness of your ministry and student culture.
      • Must be clear and well articulated so that no one is confused.

D-Team #3–
Next Year: Just For You

Objective

Explain to your D-Team that your student ministry is a place for them to grow, to bring their friends, to build the church, and to impact the world. In this D-Team, you will discuss what each of your students will need in order to grow in Christ.

Materials Needed

- Bibles
- Notebook and pens
- *Optional:* sticks, string, leaves, thumbtacks, and colored markers.

What Do I Need?

Have your D-Team sit down and pray together. Ask God to work through each one of you to accomplish something during this D-Team. During the next 40 minutes, have your students focus on and discuss the following question: **If this student ministry is just for me, then what do I need it to be in order for me to grow in Christ?**

To get your discussion started, suggest the following needs:

- Encouragement
- Prayer
- Commitment from everyone
- Excitement for what God is going to do
- Participation
- Support

Take out your notebook and record the needs that your students share. Keep those notes and later evaluate whether your D-Team is meeting those declared needs. If the discussion starts to get selfish and demanding, redirect your students by asking: **Is what you are asking for something that will help you grow in Christ, and how?**

Optional

Have your students make a symbol to represent the "Just For You" theme. As your students discuss their needs, provide them with sticks, string, leaves, and thumbtacks. Have them tie three sticks together to make the letter "I." Then have them attach a leaf to the front to symbolize growth. Then instruct your students to write the words: "Just For You" on the "I" with the marker. Challenge them to give this symbol to someone in their D-Team or someone in the student ministry

D-Team #3–(cont.)
Next Year: Just For You

whom they want to encourage. Or you may suggest that your students shape something in the form of the letter "U" and attach grass to it to signify growth. They could give this to someone else and say, "This ministry is just for 'U' to grow in Christ."

In Closing
Have your students gather in a circle and pray for the person on their right.

Evening Activity–Concert of Prayer
A concert of prayer is a powerful and meaningful activity to have on the last night of camp. It gives students more time to focus solely on God and all that they have learned about Him during the week. The concert of prayer should include a time for worship, corporate and individual prayer, Scripture reading, and communion. The student minister and worship leader should lead students during this time. Communion should be given according to the theology and traditions of your church or organization.

This concert of prayer follows a mes-sage and D-Team where students learned about the value of vision and your ministry's particular vision. Build on this by doing some additional vision-casting of what your student ministry could be like if the vision became reality. Paint the picture once again that your ministry is "just for you" and how you and the leaders are committed to ministering to each student. At some point during this time, enlarge the vision by challenging students to realize that the ministry is for their friends, too. Remind them that they have a gift to share: the love of Jesus Christ. Ask students to pray in their D-Teams for your ministry's vision to come to life in each of their groups. Then have a few students go up front and lead the group in praying for the student ministry values mentioned in the Friday evening message. To close, commit to build the ministry together and live out the vision by forming a large circle, taking the person's hand on either side, and asking a leader and a student to pray and ask for God's blessing.

Monday

Schedule

8:00 AM   Quiet Time

9:00 AM   Breakfast

10:00 AM   Morning Session–
Graduation

11:00 AM   Team Builder #3–
Team Vision

Noon   Checkout

12:30 PM   Load Buses

1:00 PM   Buses Leave (Lunch Stop)

Monday Morning Session–Graduation

Program Cue Sheet

TIME   **PROGRAM ELEMENT**

9:50 AM   **DOORS OPEN/WALK-IN**
Select some "high-energy" Christian music.

10:00 AM   **WORSHIP**
Worship leader selects five worship choruses.

10:18 AM   **WELCOME/ INTRODUCTION**
Host welcomes students to the graduation ceremony, congratulates them, and gives a brief introduction of the drama.

10:20 AM   **DRAMA– THE WAITING ROOM**
This drama is about decision making and should be rehearsed before camp and at least once during camp. Use students who have an ability to act and would enjoy participating in this way.

10:27 AM   **GRADUATION CEREMONY**
You and/or your leadership team should give a commencement address and spiritually affirm your students. Let them know how proud you are of them

and the bright future you see for them. Remind them that "being confident of this, that he who began a good work in you will carry it on to completion until the day of Christ Jesus" (Philippians 1:6).

For the actual ceremony, begin playing "Pomp and Circumstance." Challenge those students who are ready to "graduate" and willing to commit to building the student ministry to come forward and receive their diploma. Shake each student's hand. This is a moment for you and your leaders to witness life change as students understand the ministry vision and to celebrate each student's commitment.

You may also want to write your ministry's vision on the diploma so that it reminds students of their commitment. Don't pressure students; some may not be ready or willing to step forward. It's better to know who is fully on board with you than to be wondering who is committed and who is not. Some new students may not yet fully understand your ministry; be patient and make sure they stay connected after camp.

10:50 AM SONG
Have a vocalist sing, or play a CD of a song focused on commitment.

10:54 AM ANNOUNCEMENTS AND DISMISS
Host should share any closing announcements and give instructions for departure. He or she should close in prayer and thank God for how He worked in students' hearts and the many things He taught the group about building a student ministry.

Drama Script–
The Waiting Room

Scene opens in a room with several different types of chairs at different angles and different heights. Dianne sits working on a crossword puzzle. Ann sits paging through a magazine. Ian lays across his chair with this hand on his head as if in pain. Dan, dressed in a tuxedo, enters, looks around, and begins pacing. There is a phone on a small table in the center of the room. Dan picks it up, listens, and then puts it down quickly ... paces again.

Dianne: (to Dan) A little nervous, are you?

Dan: Huh? Oh, no ... just impatient. I hate waiting. ...

Dianne: Like, we don't!

Ann: It's a total waste of time, I mean, you can't get anything productive done ... because you don't know how much time you've got ... so you can't really start something ... because you're not sure if you'll be able to finish it or not. (sighs) It's so frustrating.

Dan: (confused) Yeah, well, like I said ... I hate waiting.

Ian: (moans) Not as much as I do.

Ann: (sarcastic) Oh yes, I guess *we* shouldn't complain.

Dan: (to Ian) Do you have a headache? Do you want some aspirin or something?

Dianne: No, nothing seems to help him.

Dan: Oh, sorry. (breaking an uncomfortable silence) Who ... who was here first?

Dianne: I was, why?

Dan: Am I supposed to take a number somewhere? (to Ann) Do you have a number?

Ann: A number? What for?

Dan: To know when it's your turn!

Dianne: We don't take turns.

Dan: Well, just how far behind schedule are we ... a half hour ... an hour?

Ian: (irritated) There isn't any schedule, dude.

Dan: What do you mean? There has to be a schedule ... when do we find out ... what we came to find out?

Dianne: There is no order.

Ann: None that we've seen, anyway.

Dan: Are you kidding?

Ian: Do I look like she's kidding?

Dan: Well, there must be some kind of ... ranking of needs ... I mean, I'm supposed to pick Jill up for the prom in two hours! My problem is urgent!

Ann: So is mine!

Dianne: And mine! And certainly so is his! (points to Ian, he moans)

Dan: (sits, having been put in his place) Oh. (a long pause, to Dianne) So, how long have you been waiting?

Dianne: Four years.

Dan: (jumps up and shouts) FOUR YEARS!!!!

Ian: (moans) Keep it down, will ya?

Dan: What are you waiting for?

Dianne: (a bit uncomfortable) Well, to make a long story short ... I'm waiting for my friend ... or ex-friend Amy. We both liked the same guy in eighth grade and well, when he seemed to be interested in me, not her, she told him some "confidential" things about me ... and well, then I told him some "confidential" things about her ... and well, neither of us wound up going out with him. We haven't spoken to each other since. I miss her ... her birthday is next week.

Dan: So what are you waiting for?

Dianne: I just told you ... I'm waiting for her to call.

Dan: Why don't you just call her?

Dianne: (look of horror) Because I'm waiting for her to call me! If she calls, that will show me that I should take the next step to make things right.

Dan: Huh?

Dianne: Yeah, my signal that I should do something. I hate waiting too, but it's a whole lot better than doing something stupid and being really embarrassed.

Dan: But it's been four years!

Dianne: Four years without a mistake!

Ann: (after a pause) She's right, you know.

Dan: How long have you been waiting?

Ann: Almost a year.

Dan: You've wasted a whole year of your life here ... waiting for a phone call?

Ann: Look, my parents got divorced last year. I don't feel like I belong anywhere or to anyone. I'm not gonna decide which one to live with, or who's church to go to ... or any of that. I don't want to end up like my brother.

Dan: What happened to him?

Dianne: He went to live with our father, his grades started dropping, and the counselor at school suggested he be hospitalized for depression.

Ann: And that's not going to happen to me ... I mean, I want to do the right thing and act the right way and know that no one is going to get hurt before I just walk out there. ...

Dan: But that's crazy ... you're never going to be able to ...

Ann: No! I'm waiting for my call ... my guarantee ... first.

Dan: (frustrated, to Ian) So, what about you?

Ian: What about me?

Dan: How long have you been waiting?

Ian: Ever since I was kicked out, three weeks ago.

Dan: Kicked out?

Ian: Yeah, my coach kicked me off the team because I wouldn't get help.

Dan: What do you mean, help?

Ian: He thinks I have a drinking problem.

Ann: He only plays well when he's drunk.

Dianne: He's only happy when he's high.

Ian: (mad) Yeah, well, it ain't my fault, and besides, it's not as bad as they say it is. Anyway, Coach said I can come back as soon as I've made some progress.

Dan: So, have you seen anyone?

Ian: No.

Dan: Why not? What are you waiting for?

Ian: For my coach to call me and tell me I can come back ... the team needs me. I don't need no help ... I can stop anytime I want.

Dianne: He's been saying that since he got here.

Dan: (to Ian) But why don't you call and get some help? And you (to Ann), why don't you talk to someone at your church or even your pastor and see what your

options are ... (to Dianne) And four years, my word, certainly you could call your friend. ...

Ian: (after a long pause) Why don't you?

Dan: Why don't I what?

Ian: Just go pick up your date for the prom ... and go!

Dan: Well, I ... well, maybe I will ... it's just not so easy these days ... you know, the prom itself isn't the problem ... it's after the prom–what you have to do after the prom. I mean, everybody is getting hotel rooms now and sleeping together and I'm not sure I'm ready ... or that I even should ... I mean there are lots of conse-quences and well, what will my friends think if I don't? This is a big decision I'm facing!

Ian: So is mine!

Ann: And mine!

Dianne: And so is mine!

Ann: (Dan is staring at the phone, pause) So, how long do you plan to wait?

Dan: Until I get a clearer picture ... Until I know ... I'm not making ... the wrong decision ... (pause) How often does it ring?

Dianne: Ring? (looks at the others) I don't know, we haven't heard it yet.

Blackout

Team Builder #3–
Team Vision

In this Team Builder, you and the leaders on your team will have a chance to communicate the "Just For You" vision for your team and what that really means for your particular team for the rest of the ministry season. Each team will have a unique way to carry out this vision. Therefore, the agenda needs to be determined by each team's leaders.

Camp Follow-up

- Show pictures or video highlights of the camp at your next student program.
- Follow up on new students who came to the camp and make sure they stay connected in the ministry.
- Follow up immediately on students who made decisions to trust Christ.
- Use the momentum generated at the camp and keep building on it by meeting together on a regular basis.
- Continue teaching topics related to what was taught at the camp and casting the ministry vision.
- Use the phrase "Just For You" at your programs. Make a banner with "Just For You" on it and hang it where students can see it and be reminded of how your ministry desires to serve them.
- Offer "graduate school" for those students who "graduated" from Impact University by occasionally meeting with them apart from the rest of the group to teach them more about the ministry's vision, mission, and strategy.
- Encourage leaders to continue building relationships with the students in their small groups and to check on areas in which students committed to grow, especially in the five Gs.
- Provide opportunities for students to maintain the bonds they built by implementing or continuing a small group ministry and placing students on campus teams.
- Evaluate the camp by asking the following questions:
  Did the facility serve us well? Would we go there again?
  Did we promote the camp far enough in advance?
  How did students respond to the speaker? Would we ask him or her to speak at next year's camp?
  Did the programming elements flow together smoothly?
  How did we do financially? Do we need to budget more money next year?
  Was the schedule too packed or was there the right amount of free time?
  Did we have the right leaders and enough volunteers to help?
  What did we learn?
  How can next year's camp be better?
- Write thank-you notes to your leaders, speaker, and musicians.
- Call or write the campsite and thank the personnel for their help in making your camp run smoothly.
- Take time to celebrate with your staff and/or leadership team the amazing things God did at the camp.
- Rest!

Student Notes # 1
What Kind of Ministry?

Read the statements in each row. Then circle the statement that is most true of your D-Team within our ministry.

Column A	Column B
• My D-Team is made up primarily of students who are spectators when it comes to God's work.	• The students in my D-Team participate in serving God actively.
• The students in my D-Team get very excited about different activities we do as a group that are fun and entertaining.	• The students in my D-Team get fired up about seeing ministry happen to their friends.
• The students in my D-Team rarely invite non-Christian friends. In fact, we don't have many non-Christian friends.	• The students in my D-Team have compassion for their friends and friendships with non-Christians.
• I often feel as if members of my D-Team come because they are forced to attend, or because it's a great place to socialize.	• The students in my D-Team attend because they want to and because they want to see how God is working.
• The students in my D-Team complain a lot about our group, wishing we were more united.	• The students in my D-Team are involved in making the necessary changes to make our group better.
• Most of the time, the leaders run my D-Team. There's not much student participation in planning.	• The students in my D-Team take ownership, and I feel that they sense that the ministry is partly theirs.
• The students in my D-Team attend whenever it's convenient for them.	• The students in my D-Team are committed.
• The students in my D-Team are not available to participate because they do not see the D-Team as a priority.	• The students in my D-Team are available, responsive, and willing participants.
• The students in my D-Team are bored with the teaching of God's Word.	• The students in my D-Team are teachable and excited to learn more of God's Word.
• The students in my D-Team see no ultimate purpose beyond fellowship for our D-Team.	• The students in my D-Team have a vision for reaching the lost on their campus.
• The students in my D-Team like their Christian friends, but do not challenge each other's spiritual growth.	• The students in my D-Team intentionally challenge and encourage each other spiritually.

Student Notes #2
Saturday Morning Quiet Time

This is your first morning at camp. The rush of last night is probably still heavy on your eyes! But there is Someone who would like to start out the day with you. He would love to hear your voice and show you His goodness in return. Take the time to meet with your Lord and King this morning before the excitement of the day gets the best of you. If possible, take a walk and quietly read the following psalm.

Psalm 145

I will exalt you, my God the King; I will praise your name for ever and ever. Every day I will praise you and extol your name for ever and ever.
Great is the LORD and most worthy of praise; his greatness no one can fathom.
One generation will commend your works to another; they will tell of your mighty acts.
They will speak of the glorious splendor of your majesty, and I will meditate on your wonderful works.
They will tell of the power of your awesome works, and I will proclaim your great deeds.
They will celebrate your abundant goodness and joyfully sing of your righteousness.
The LORD is gracious and compassionate, slow to anger and rich in love.
The LORD is good to all; he has compassion on all he has made.
All you have made will praise you, O LORD; your saints will extol you.
They will tell of the glory of your kingdom and speak of your might, so that all men may know of your mighty acts and the glorious splendor of your kingdom.
Your kingdom is an everlasting kingdom, and your dominion endures through all generations.
The LORD is faithful to all his promises and loving toward all he has made. The LORD upholds all those who fall and lifts up all who are bowed down.
The eyes of all look to you, and you give them their food at the proper time.
You open your hand and satisfy the desires of every living thing.
The LORD is righteous in all his ways and loving toward all he has made.
The LORD is near to all who call on him, to all who call on him in truth.
He fulfills the desires of those who fear him; he hears their cry and saves them.
The LORD watches over all who love him, but all the wicked he will destroy.
My mouth will speak in praise of the LORD.
Let every creature praise his holy name for ever and ever.

Reread the psalm and substitute *I* wherever you see the word *they*. Then ask yourself, *Will I do all these things?* Pick one part of the psalm that you have a hard time personalizing because you know it isn't true in your life. For instance, do you tell of the power of God's awesome works or call on Him? Take some time to praise Him and then thank Him for all His blessings in your life. To close your time with the King, share with Him about what you learned this morning. May you see His face and know that He is God today.

The Five Gs

Grace
- Have you ever accepted God's grace into your life? When and where?
- What does your grace gauge look like? Do you accept God's grace daily in your life? Do you extend that grace to other people around you? Why or why not?
- Maybe this is the "G" that you need to work through in your life. Ask your D-Team members to support you in this area of your life.

Growth
- Prayer, worship, and Bible study are vital elements in deepening one's walk with Christ. Are you presently nurturing your spiritual growth privately through those spiritual disciplines? How often, and what are you doing?
- In your pursuit of becoming more Christlike, what areas are most difficult for you?
- What does your growth gauge look like? Do you see it as being low or high at this point in your life?
- Maybe this is the "G" that you need to work through in your life. Ask your D-Team members to support you in this area of your life.

Group
- Do you regularly participate in the corporate gatherings of your ministry? Why or why not?
- Are you connected to a small group of believers for the purpose of growth, loving support, and accountability? Why or why not?
- What does your group gauge look like? Do you see it as balanced in this area, or do you need to make some changes?
- Maybe this is the "G" that you need to work through in your life. Ask your D-Team members to support you in this area of your life.

Gifts
- Are you interested in finding out what spiritual gifts God has given you to use in a place of service within the church?
- Are you currently finding out what your gifts are?
- If you already know what your spiritual gifts are, are you presently using them in an area of service within your youth ministry? Within another ministry at your church? If not, why not?
- What does your gifts gauge look like? Do you feel as though you are pursuing your gifts to the best of your ability?
- Maybe this is the "G" that you need to work through in your life. Ask your D-Team members to support you in this area of your life.

Good Stewardship
- Do you regularly support this youth ministry using 10 percent as a goal to reach?
- What does your stewardship gauge look like? Do you see it resting in the healthy range in your life right now?
- Maybe this is the "G" that you need to work through in your life. Ask your D-Team members to support you in this area of your life.

Student Notes #4
Sunday Morning Quiet Time

This morning's challenge is to see God through the eyes of David, the writer of Psalm 103. Relax and enjoy the company of your Maker and your Friend. If possible, sit outside and take in what He has created for you.

Psalm 103

Praise the LORD, O my soul; all my inmost being, praise his holy name.
Praise the LORD, O my soul, and forget not all his benefits—
who forgives all your sins and heals all your diseases,
who redeems your life from the pit
and crowns you with love and compassion,
who satisfies your desires with good things
so that your youth is renewed like the eagle's.
The LORD works righteousness and justice for all the oppressed.
He made known his ways to Moses, his deeds to the people of Israel:
The LORD is compassionate and gracious, slow to anger, abounding in love.
He will not always accuse, nor will he harbor his anger forever;
he does not treat us as our sins deserve or repay us according to our iniquities.
For as high as the heavens are above the earth,
so great is his love for those who fear him;
as far as the east is from the west,
so far has he removed our transgressions from us.
As a father has compassion on his children,
so the LORD has compassion on those who fear him;
for he knows how we are formed, he remembers that we are dust.
As for man, his days are like grass, he flourishes like a flower of the field;
the wind blows over it and it is gone, and its place remembers it no more.
But from everlasting to everlasting
the LORD's love is with those who fear him,
and his righteousness with their children's children—
with those who keep his covenant and remember to obey his precepts.
The LORD has established his throne in heaven,
and his kingdom rules over all.
Praise the LORD, you his angels, you mighty ones who do his bidding,
who obey his word.
Praise the LORD, all his heavenly hosts, you his servants who do his will.
Praise the LORD, all his works everywhere in his dominion.
Praise the LORD, O my soul.

Did you experience God's presence through this psalm? If so, in what way? If not, how will you pursue Him today?

Student Notes #5
Monday Morning Quiet Time

This is the last morning that you will have here at camp. Maybe you haven't taken the time to be with your heavenly Father yet this weekend, but now you desire to seek His face. Or maybe you have been meeting with Him every morning, and it has been refreshing for you. By now you should have learned that if you seek Him, you will find Him. No matter what the circumstances–He is waiting to commune with you. He wants to hear your voice and what you have learned about Him over the past three days. He wants to celebrate with you and encourage you.

Take about 10–15 minutes to reflect on the past few days. Then write down the truths that you have learned about God and His wonderful works.

Now take a few minutes to thank God for what He has shown you. Pray aloud, if possible. Sometimes praying aloud helps us stay focused on what we are saying.

Lastly, read Proverbs 2:1–15 and 3:1–6. Record what God intends for you to do with what you have learned about Him.

Optional
If you want to show someone that you learned something significant about Jesus and how that truth relates to you, then write a note telling that person about it. It could be a friend, D-Team leader, or the Campus Director. Just encourage someone else's pursuit of God by telling them what you are learning.

MISSION

Retreat Summary: This weekend retreat is named after the movie and TV show, *Mission: Impossible*. Students will learn that they each were created in the image of God and have been created for a specific mission. Every student will be challenged and given the opportunity to decide if they will accept and carry out their God-given missions.

Length of Retreat: Friday night through Sunday afternoon.

Target Audience: Seekers and believers. Seekers will learn that God has a plan for every person and that salvation is a mission that is possible for them. Believers will identify their unique God-given missions and learn that with God, all things are possible.

Facility Requirements: Ideal setting would be cabins or a retreat center. A large meeting room is needed for programs.

Retreat Objectives:
- To assist students in identifying their unique missions from God.
- To give students time to listen to God.
- To teach students that all things are possible with God.
- To help students build relationships and memories.

Introduction: The Bible is filled with men and women who were called by God to fulfill unique missions. Moses was called by God from a burning bush to lead the Israelites out of Egypt. Nehemiah's mission was to rebuild the city wall. Esther's mission was to save the Jews. Her cousin, Mordecai, sent the following message to her: "And who knows but that you have come to royal position for such a time as this?" (Esther 4:14). Jonah's mission was to evangelize Nineveh. Mary was asked by God to bear His Son. God gave Paul the vision to launch the first church.

God is still looking for men and women to stand in the gap for Him so that He can use them to impact the world. Your mission, should you choose to accept it, is to help your students understand that God is still assigning missions to those who are willing to submit their hearts and follow Him today. This introduction will self-destruct in five seconds. Good luck!

Retreat Checklist

ACTIVITIES
___ Elements for communion

COMPETITION
___ Cones and flags for Capture the Flag

D-TEAMS
___ Pens and paper
___ Bottle of water for each student
___ White labels and markers
___ Mission Cards

EMERGENCIES
___ First Aid kit
___ Names and phone numbers of each camper's parent or guardian
___ Name and directions to nearest hospital from campsite

HANDOUTS AND SUPPLIES
___ Student notebooks
___ Copies of Student Notes #1, #2, #3, and #4
___ Leader Responsibility Sheets
___ Extra Bibles
___ Camera and/or video

PROGRAMS
___ Musical instruments
___ Props for stage
___ *Mission: Impossible* video
___ Walk-in music as students enter program
___ Song sheets or slides for worship choruses
___ Recording of "Go and Sin No More" by Rebecca St. James (*God*, ForeFront, 1996) for the Concert of Prayer.

REGISTRATION
___ Completed permission slips from each camper and leader
___ Room assignments
___ Petty cash box to collect remaining payments for the retreat

VEHICLES
___ Maps to campsite
___ Insurance documents
___ Money for gas and tolls

This is a sample letter we gave to all D-Team leaders at a meeting prior to camp. Along with this letter, leaders also received D-Team material to study and prepare.

Dear D-Team Leader:

After many weeks of prayer, preparation, and trying to get your students to turn in their registration forms, Mission Impossible is almost here. As you think about the upcoming camp, you probably feel a sense of anticipation as well as nervousness. Take a deep breath and relax–you don't have to lead on your own. Relying on the Holy Spirit is the most important thing you can do as you lead your students during the retreat.

Your mission over the weekend, should you choose to accept it, is to lead the students in your D-Team into a deeper understanding of their individual God-given missions. Through solitude, prayer, study of God's Word, and D-Team discussions, students will identify the unique mission God has in store for them and the action they need to take on it. You are the agent God has selected to help these students.

Take time before the retreat to prepare yourself spiritually. Ask God how He could best use you and the gifts He has given you. Set aside time this week to listen to how God wants you to lead and shepherd the students He has entrusted to your care. Spend time praying for the students in your D-Team, asking God to draw them closer to Him. Also, pray that

- the students who have not yet accepted Christ will come to know Him at this camp.
- the students who are trying D-Teams out for the first time will have a positive experience.
- the students will understand their God-given missions and develop action steps to carry those missions out.
- the message givers will communicate God's Word clearly and will be empowered by Him.
- there will be safety in travel.
- our ministry will receive protection.
- our leaders will have direction, discernment, and strength.

During Mission Impossible, you will have the privilege of leading the students in your D-Team and helping them to become fully devoted followers of Christ. Your D-Team should sit together during mealtimes, the main sessions, and at the Concert of Prayer. Because you will be together during these sessions, you will have the opportunity to be creative and "own" your meeting area by decorating it or bringing notes or small gifts to your students each session.

The D-Team material will give you all the information and ideas you will need to lead your D-Team throughout the week. There are also leadership meetings scheduled each day to keep you informed of the day's activities and also to answer any questions you may have. The following checklist will help you remember your main responsibilities for each session:

- Be prepared spiritually. Set aside time to pray and listen to God.
- Bring something to decorate your meeting area for each session.
  Possible ideas: personal notes, candy, gum, pictures, magnifying glass, small tape recorder, etc. Be creative!
- Study the D-Team curriculum before you arrive at camp. You will find suggested questions and Scripture to use in each D-Team, so familiarize yourself with the material.
- Encourage students to be on time to all sessions and to bring their notebooks and Bibles. Lead by example.

Our time together is going to be incredible! Thank you for your commitment and passion to see high school students grow into fully devoted followers of Christ. Your role is so important and we greatly value and appreciate you. It will be exciting to serve together with you and to witness the amazing ways God is going to work through you to impact students' lives! This letter will self-destruct in five seconds. Good luck!

Retreat Overview

Theme

In the movie *Mission: Impossible*, agents are given risky and adventurous missions to complete. These missions are given on tapes that self-destruct after they are reviewed. Using this idea, give your leaders special instructions and training on tape to be listened to prior to the retreat.

Handouts

Every student should be given some kind of handout or notebook to use for taking notes or journaling. You may want to include your retreat schedule in this handout as well as camp rules, a camp map, and information on various issues. Encourage students to bring their notebooks to all sessions and D-Teams.

Here are a few ideas for designing your student notebook:

- Develop written material and print into booklet form.
- Make stickers with the camp logo and stick them onto plain, inexpensive notebooks.
- Screen the camp logo onto 5 1/2" x 8 1/2" three-ring notebooks and build this expense into camp costs.

Take-Away

Consider giving your students some kind of tangible reminder of their retreat experience and how God worked. The take-away for this retreat could be the Mission Cards each student will receive in D-Team #2. You could make them in two different sizes: one to tape to a mirror at home and one small enough to fit in a wallet.

Schedule

A sample daily schedule used by Student Impact for Mission Impossible is included as a guideline to help you develop your own schedule. While schedules can be restrictive at times, they will keep your leaders and students organized each day and help make your time together purposeful.

Missions

Missions in this retreat are like scavenger hunts, designed to build unity among D-Teams and campus teams. If your campsite is large, it may be helpful to give students a map. You will find specific instructions on pages 127 and 140 for each mission. You may want to add or change the clues based on your campsite and group. Be careful not to put students in dangerous situations or risk injury. Explain to students that these missions are a race against the clock, but property should not be destroyed in an effort to win. Offer prizes to the winning team each day.

Competition

Brainstorm with your leadership team a competitive activity that all your students will enjoy participating in on Saturday afternoon. It's fun to offer some kind of competition that will determine a winner so that you can announce the camp champions.

A suggested idea for competition that is in keeping with the retreat theme is to play Capture the Flag. You will find game instructions on page 132.

D-Teams

D-Teams (small groups) give students a

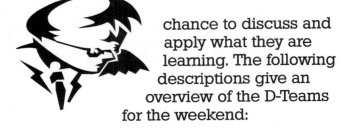

chance to discuss and apply what they are learning. The following descriptions give an overview of the D-Teams for the weekend:

D-Team #1–Be Still and Know
During this D-Team, students will learn about and have the opportunity to practice the discipline of solitude. They will be challenged to determine in which areas of their personal lives God wants them to grow or change.

D-Team #2–My Mission
During this D-Team, students will identify their personal missions and determine how they are going to accomplish them.

Programs

All programming elements are designed to move each student emotionally and intellectually to see God's love by exposing God's truth in a relevant, practical way through the communicative arts. Each program points students toward a basic biblical truth. Sample Cue Sheets include suggested program orders.

Here are a few ideas, materials, and props you may want to use in planning your programs:

Ideas
1. Watch *Mission: Impossible* with your planning team and take notes on scenes you could reenact.
2. Watch *The Saint* or some James Bond spy movies to generate ideas.
3. Dress leaders or musical band members as spies. Ask them to wear trench coats and sunglasses. The person who gives announcements could also dress as a spy and carry a briefcase.

Materials/Props
Our stage set was quite simple. We used laser beams to spotlight the audience and special lighting to add intrigue. Of course, we played the *Mission: Impossible* theme song throughout the weekend. You can find this song on the movie soundtrack CD, *Mission: Impossible* (Mother Records, 1996).

Messages

Four messages are included in this retreat. Try to make all of your teaching times interactive and creative. Use the material provided, but take time to hear what the Holy Spirit wants to communicate to your students through you.

Student Impact's speaker for this retreat was the Rev. Harvey Carey, youth pastor of Salem Baptist Church of Chicago, Illinois. Here are brief summaries of the evening and morning messages:

Friday Evening Message–What Is a Mission?
Students will learn what God says about mission and purpose.

Saturday Morning Message–You Have a Mission
Students will understand that each Christian has been given a particular mission from God.

Saturday Evening Message–Discovering Your Mission
Students will learn how to discover their individual mission from God.

Sunday Morning Message–A Mission with Power
Students will be challenged and reminded that the Gospel of Jesus Christ can change their lives and also their friends' lives.

Friday

Schedule

5:00 PM   Registration

6:00 PM   Buses Leave

8:00 PM   Arrive at Camp

9:00 PM   Evening Session–
What Is a Mission?

10:15 PM   Evening Activity–
Mission #1

11:15 PM   Room Check

12:00 AM   Lights Out

Friday Evening Session Program Cue Sheet

TIME	PROGRAM ELEMENT
9:00 PM	**DOORS OPEN/WALK-IN** Play some "high-energy" Christian music.
9:05 PM	**SONG** Select a contemporary Christian song to kick off the retreat.
9:10 PM	**WELCOME/ ANNOUNCEMENTS** Host (dressed as a spy) welcomes everyone and states the retreat rules including the 3 Ms: • Be at all **m**eals. • Be at all **m**eetings.

• Be **m**odest in all you do and say.

9:15 PM	**WORSHIP** Worship leader selects 15 minutes' worth of "up-tempo" celebrative songs. (See Appendix C for a list of choruses.)
9:20 PM	**INTRODUCTION OF WEEK-END THEME AND SPEAKER** Host introduces the weekend theme and the speaker for the evening.
9:35 PM	**MESSAGE– WHAT IS A MISSION?** See Friday Evening Message rationale and outline.
10:05 PM	**ANNOUNCEMENTS AND DISMISSAL** Host prays and gives the schedule for Saturday.

Friday Evening Message–
What Is a Mission?

Big Idea
"Mission" is very similar to "purpose." This message is designed to help students understand the definition of mission and purpose. Purpose is the reason that something or someone exists and mission is the carrying out of that purpose. (Scriptural basis: John 5:30; Habakkuk 2:2–3)

Rationale
We can know our mission by understanding two things:
1. The definition of mission and purpose.
2. Mission gives meaning and reason to life.

Message Outline
I. Introduction
   We often follow the patterns and behaviors of the "coolest" people around. This is one of the perils of peer pressure. We want so badly to be like them and to associate with them. Out of all the "cool" people who ever lived, Jesus wins hands down! As we attempt to find our identity and place in this world, we should look to the life of Christ. Read John 5:30–Jesus was a man of purpose.

II. The Value of Mission and Purpose
   a. Mission and purpose are God's intent for our creation.
   b. Mission is not defined by the secular world, but by the Word of God.
      • God intends for us to find His purpose for our lives.
      • Illustration: Imagine you have a garment bag with wheels; but every time you use it at the airport, you struggle to carry your luggage. One day you watch a man use the same garment bag with ease. Why? He used it properly by lifting the handle up and using the wheels to pull the garment bag. This prompts you to stop struggling and to pull up the handle on your own piece of luggage. Point: In life, we all have gifts, talents, and abilities. When we are ignorant of what those things are, we often struggle through life.
      • Read Habakkuk 2:2–3 and state that vision gives life a track on which to run!

III. Mission gives life meaning and reason.
   a. Where purpose is not known, abuse is inevitable.
   b. Known purpose makes life much easier!

IV. Conclusion
   Challenge students to seek God about the reason and purpose for their lives. Close in a prayer of dedication, thanking God that purpose is a part of His plan for each of us.

Evening Activity–
Mission #1

Mission #1 gives students an opportunity to build community with others from their campus team or small group (depending on how you choose to divide up students for this exercise) and a chance to have fun together. Give each campus team or small group a copy of Student Notes #1–Mission #1.

To complete CODE: 8.22.96.1A, students must write down the model and make of the transportation (bus, car, or van) used to get to camp. The coded numbers should be the current date.

To complete CODE: 8.22.96.2A, students must write down all the names of the dorms or cabins where they are staying and the year each building was built, if available.

To complete CODE: 8.22.96.3A, students must find golf or tennis balls on the playing field or in the recreation center and bring one back as proof that they accomplished their mission.

As teams show up at mission headquarters, check the answers on their list and keep track of which team was the fastest and most accurate. Award a prize to the winning team and let teams know that another mission awaits them on Sunday morning.

Saturday

Schedule

7:45 AM	Leaders' Meeting
8:00 AM	Breakfast
9:00 AM	Morning Session–**You Have a Mission**
10:30 AM	D-Team #1–**Be Still and Know**
12:00 PM	Lunch
1:30 PM	Competition
3:00 PM	Free Time
5:00 PM	Dinner
6:00 PM	One-on-Ones
7:00 PM	Evening Session–**Discovering Your Mission**
8:30 PM	D-Team #2–**My Mission**
10:00 PM	Concert of Prayer
11:00 PM	Snack
11:45 PM	Room Check
12:00 AM	Lights Out

Saturday Morning Session Program Cue Sheet

TIME	PROGRAM ELEMENT
8:45 AM	**DOORS OPEN/WALK-IN** Play some "high-energy" Christian music.
9:02 AM	**SONG** Have a vocalist sing or play a CD of a song about following Christ.
9:06 AM	**WORSHIP** Worship leader conducts 15 minutes of "up-tempo" and medium tempo worship choruses that focus on God's work in our lives.
9:21 AM	**INTRODUCTION OF MORNING TOPIC** Host introduces the morning theme.
9:26 AM	**MESSAGE– YOU HAVE A MISSION** See Saturday Morning Message rationale and outline.
9:56 AM	**ANNOUNCEMENTS** Host (dressed as a spy) explains the rest of the day's schedule and dismisses students to D-Team #1.

Saturday Morning Message–
You Have a Mission

Big Idea
Students need to know that each of them has been given a unique mission from God. They not only have individual missions (which are often connected to others within the body of Christ), but they also have corporate missions, such as evangelism. (Scriptural basis: Ecclesiastes 3:1; Jeremiah 1:5–10)

Rationale
We can learn about our missions by realizing two truths:
1. All people are born with a mission.
2. Our individual missions merge with the corporate body of Christ.

Message Outline
I. Introduction
    Necessity is the mother of invention. Heat and sweating necessitated the invention of the fan, and lengthy travel necessitated the invention of the car, plane, and space shuttle. Tell students that their existence means that there is a need or necessity that only they can answer or solve. Their existence was planned and purposed by God; they are not an accident or merely a biological result. Each of them is a part of God's eternal plan.
    a. Read Ecclesiastes 3:1 and explain that there is a purpose to everything under heaven. Students do have a mission and purpose!
    b. Read Jeremiah 1:5–10 and explain the importance of being young with purpose and mission.

II. All People Are Born with a Mission.
    a. Mission is given before birth.
    b. Birth is proof of the mission's importance to God.
    c. Mission does not discriminate by age.
        • Cite examples from the Bible of how God used young people such as David, Jeremiah, Mary (mother of Jesus), and Timothy.

III. Our Individual Missions Merge with the Corporate Body of Christ.
    a. God uses our missions together to create His overall purpose. No man is an island. Our mission is ultimately for His purpose!
    b. God causes our understanding of mission to ignite a desire for knowledge of purpose in them.
    c. The Great Commission is our overall purpose (both individually and as a body of believers).

IV. Conclusion
    We all share one common mission: evangelism. We are called to evangelize regardless of age, economic background, or social conditions. We can share the good news of Christ individually and as a group!

D-Team #1 –
Be Still and Know

Objective
During this first D-Team, students will be given an opportunity to spend some time in solitude to determine in which areas of their personal lives God wants them to grow or change. This time spent in solitude will hopefully help students begin to identify their God-given mission.

Key Verse
"But when you pray, go into your room, close the door and pray to your Father, who is unseen. Then your Father, who sees what is done in secret, will reward you" (Matthew 6:6).

Materials Needed
- Bibles
- Pens
- Paper
- Copies of Student Notes #2

The Message
Say, "In a few minutes, we're going to read 1 Kings 19:9–13 and answer the questions on Student Notes #2. Earlier in this chapter, we learn that the prophet Elijah's life had been threatened and he had escaped into the desert. He may have been facing a crisis of faith, identity, or vision. After being sustained by the angel of the Lord, Elijah journeyed to Mt. Horeb. Now, let's take a look at how God appeared to Elijah."

Discuss the following questions with your D-Team:

Where did God find Elijah? (In a cave in Mt. Horeb.)

Why do you think God asked Elijah, "What are you doing here?" (The question may imply that Elijah had come to the mountain for his own reasons rather than because God had sent him there.)

How did Elijah answer God's question? (Elijah did not give a direct answer. Instead he implied that God's initiation of the covenant had amounted to nothing since the Israelites had broken it.)

How did God respond to Elijah's complaints that his work was fruitless? (God invited Elijah to experience His presence by coming out of the cave and standing on the mountain.)

After hearing God's invitation, what would you expect to happen next? (Allow your students to share their ideas.)

If you were standing there with Elijah, and the wind came and tore up the mountain, would you naturally assume it was God trying to get your attention? Or if that didn't move you, what about the earthquake or fire? After all that commotion, would you even pay attention to the whisper? (There are no right or wrong answers. Listen to your students and be honest with how *you* would respond.)

Why do you think God did not present Himself to Elijah in the wind, earthquake, and fire? (Remind your D-Team that the whole reason Elijah was in trouble with King Ahab and Queen Jezebel was because he had defeated their prophets of Baal by asking God to rain

down fire on the sacrifice at Mt. Carmel. Perhaps God was trying to tell Elijah that though the Israelites might have deserved His wrath and judgment through winds, earthquakes, and fires, that was not His will. God's whisper may have symbolized His gift of grace and guidance for Elijah as He called him to continue His mission to the Israelites.)

After discussing the questions on Student Notes #2, say, **"We don't have '40 days' to reach God this weekend, but we can take the first steps to establish the discipline of sorting through the winds, earthquakes, and fires in our lives. We can begin listening for the whispers of God when they come to our hearts."**

Instruct your students to find a quiet corner or go somewhere that is quiet and free of distractions so they can read the Reflection in their Student Notes. Ask your student to return in 20 minutes for a debriefing. Before sending students off by themselves, pray for each one of them individually.

Spend the next 20 minutes alone praying for your students. Ask God to speak to their hearts. Also, ask God for wisdom to help you sort through the lists that your students will come back with.

Debrief

As your students return from their solitude walk, start talking about the lists that they compiled. Ask them if they can eliminate the outside daily distractions. Then encourage them to circle one or two inner struggles that they think God is trying to talk to them about. Some of your students may need individual help, but if it is appropriate, ask the D-Team to help sort through their lists.

There is no need to narrow these struggles down. Assure your D-Team that at a later session, they will be asked to write down the areas of their lives that they would like to make as their missions. At that time, if they haven't picked one, they will be instructed to do so.

In Closing

Close in prayer, asking God to prepare your students throughout the day for the next message and D-Team experience where they will be making some important decisions about their lives.

Saturday Afternoon Competition–
Capture the Flag

Number of players needed: 8 and up and divided into two teams (countries).

Equipment needed: 1 flag for each team and cones or ropes to mark boundaries.

Objective: To steal the enemy's flag and bring it safely back to your team's side while avoiding capture and imprisonment behind enemy lines.

This game can be played in large or small areas and requires minimal equipment. To play, divide players into two teams, or "countries," and determine boundaries for each "country." Mark out a prison on each side and have each team display its flag on its own side. Each team must develop its own strategy and divide into offensive and defensive units. The defenders stay behind to guard their team's flag, while the offenders go behind enemy lines and try to steal the enemy's flag. A defender captures an invader by holding him or her long enough to say *Caught* three times. A captured player remains in prison until a teammate runs through his or her cell shouting *Free!* three times. The first team to capture the enemy flag and bring it home wins the game.

To fit with the Mission Impossible theme, you could call this game "Capture the Mission List" and use a manila folder or other form of paper instead of a flag. A variation to this game involves a twist on prison. When an invader is caught, the defender brings the prisoner before the prison warden (you or one of your leaders positioned in the center of the playing field). The prison warden determines the "punishment" and what the prisoner must do to be freed. Some examples of "punishment" could be: 20 push-ups; a rendition of "Row, Row, Row Your Boat"; reciting a retreat theme Bible verse; 5 somersaults. It makes getting caught a bit more fun!

Saturday
Evening Session

Program Cue Sheet

TIME	PROGRAM ELEMENT
6:45 PM	**DOORS OPEN/WALK-IN** Play some "high-energy" Christian music.
7:05 PM	**WELCOME AND INTRODUCTION** Host shares a personal story about how he or she discovered his or her mission and what that mission entailed.
7:10 PM	**WORSHIP** Worship leader conducts 20 minutes' worth of songs that connect with the message topic.
7:30 PM	**MESSAGE– DISCOVERING YOUR MISSION** See Saturday Evening Message rationale and outline.
8:05 PM	**ANNOUNCEMENTS AND DISMISSAL** Host prays, gives the schedule for the next day, and then dismisses students to D-Team #2.

Saturday Evening Message– Discovering Your Mission

Big Idea
If God has given each of us a mission, how do we know what it is? Students will learn how to discover their missions. (Scriptural basis: Jonah 1:1–3; 2:1; James 1:5)

Rationale
We can discover our mission by:
1. Seeking God.
2. Trusting God to make it known to us.
3. Being at peace.

Message Outline
I. Introduction

Imagine a young girl who is looking for a way out of a pit into which she has fallen. She is young and does not know that there is a ladder on the side that will lead her to safety. The little girl's father is looking down through the hole and trying to get the child's attention, but the child is screaming, jumping in terror, and trying to get out of the pit. Until the child calms down and listens to the voice of her father, she will never discover the way out of the pit.

During our high school years, we sometimes find ourselves in the pits of indecision and confusion. "What is my career goal? Who am I in God's plan? Should I enter full-time ministry or the marketplace after college?" The questions go on and on. We will continue to clamor in the pit of indecision until we seek our heavenly Father to find the answers.

II. Discovering our mission begins with seeking God.
Read James 1:5–God gives wisdom and understanding about life if we seek and pray to Him.
   a. Wisdom is godly understanding.
   b. Wisdom helps us to get a clear focus on our purpose.
   c. Often we know what God wants us to do, but we feel inadequate, we stubbornly rebel, or we are simply not ready to respond. Jonah is an example of someone who heard God's plan but did not want to follow. (Read Jonah 1:1–3 and 2:1.)

III. Our missions are usually made clear by God.
   a. Jonah's life parallels many Christians' lives today–known mission is often rejected.
   b. We can seek God through prayer and Scripture reading.
   Illustration: Prayer is one way to understand the mission God has given us. Pull the microphone away and speak softly to the group. Then speak into the microphone and ask the group what you said. Explain that prayer is the amplifier that takes the Word of God (words of purpose and mission) and allows us to hear them. God is always speaking–we simply have to get on His frequency!

IV. We have discovered our mission when we are at peace.
   a. Jonah received peace when he obeyed God's call. It wasn't until Jonah obeyed God that God allowed him to be at peace.
   b. We will find peace through accepting God's call. Peace is always the acid test for knowing that we are in the will of God.

V. Conclusion
Ask students to form groups of three and to pray that each of them will accept God's will for their lives.

D-Team #2–
My Mission

Objective

In this D-Team, the mission for everyone is to "love the Lord your God with all your heart," which will in turn help everyone "love your neighbor as yourself." This D-Team will help your students determine what their personal missions are and how to accomplish them.

Key Verses

"One of them, an expert in the law, tested him with this question: 'Teacher, which is the greatest commandment in the Law?' Jesus replied: 'Love the Lord your God with all your heart and with all your soul and with all your mind.' This is the first and greatest commandment. And the second is like it: 'Love your neighbor as yourself'" (Matthew 22:35–39).

Materials Needed

- Bible, notebook, and pen
- Student Notes #3
- Mission Cards (one for each student)
- Bottle of water for each student (a clear bottle to see through with a removable label)
- Plain, white labels to stick on the bottle of water (several for each student)
- Markers to write on the labels

Special Preparation

Prepare the Missions Cards with the following statement on an index card or half-sheet of paper:

I will _____

so that I can bring _____

closer to Christ.

The Message

Take the first 10–15 minutes to get one- or two-word responses from your students. Say, **"I am going to say a name and I want you to tell me what you could learn from this person's life in a word or two. For instance, for Daniel, you might respond with the words 'character,' 'stay faithful,' 'prayer is important,' 'no compromising.'"**

Noah (wisdom; have faith; patience)
Solomon (money and power aren't everything; be content; seek wisdom)
David (sin has consequences; trust God for protection)
Paul (humility; speak to others about your faith)
Joseph, son of Jacob (patience; honor; forgiveness)
Abraham (faith; obedience)
Job (endurance; seek God during trials)
Sarah (faith; patience)
Esther (courage; take risks; plan)
Miriam (leader; quick thinker)

Ask, **"Why didn't God just give us a rule book to live by? Why did He include ordinary peoples' lives and their experiences–both failures and successes–in the Bible?"** (Because we can learn valuable lessons from these biblical characters and grow in our faith. God wanted to show us what He could do through ordinary men and women. Like these biblical legends, we too can make a difference.)

Explain to your students that these people listed in Scripture loved God enough to be obedient to His will for their lives. As a result of loving God with all their hearts, they couldn't help but

influence their families, neighbors, friends, and enemies. As others observed a difference in the lives of these men and women, they were brought closer to Christ. Over 2,000 years later, these people are still changing lives because they were obedient to the mission that we are now called to carry on.

Read aloud Matthew 22:35–39. Then distribute Mission Cards to your students and explain the correlation between the Matthew 22 passage and the statement (on their Mission Cards) that they will be completing to determine their personal missions.

Say, **"Your mission is to focus on an area in your life in which you want God to work so that you can also influence a friend's life. When you love God with all your heart, He also asks that you love your neighbor."**

Reflection

Distribute copies of Student Notes #3 to your D-Team. Instruct your students to take out their copies of Student Notes #2 from the morning solitude walk. Ask, **"Have you thought through your list of distractions since this morning? Have you narrowed down what you think might be the first half of your mission? What is one of the issues or areas of your life in which God is trying to work and bring change? If it fits into the personal part of the mission, write it on your Mission Card."**

Now, have your students think for a moment about the circle of people with whom they are in contact on a daily or weekly basis. Ask, **"Within your circle of friends and acquaintances, who**

could be drawn closer to Christ as a direct result of your completing your personal mission?" Ask your students to write a specific name on the second line of their Mission Card.

Application

Hand out the water bottles, labels, and markers to your students. Help them see the purpose of their mission and how God intends to accomplish that mission with them, by using the water bottles and the following discussion. Begin by telling them that the water bottles represent their day-to-day lives.

Have a student read Matthew 23:23–28. Ask, **"Why was Jesus upset with the Pharisees?"** (The Pharisees were only worried about the appearance of doing what was right instead of actually filling their lives with Christ. If they really wanted people to grow closer to Christ, all that they would have had to do was to allow Christ to reveal Himself through them instead of working so hard to disguise their true nature and maintain rituals of outward holiness.) Ask, **"What are some of the rituals that we perform in hopes that those around us will want to know more about Christ?"** (Answers may include attending church and student ministry groups; giving the "Christian answers" to questions instead of sharing what is going on in our lives; don't drink, smoke, do drugs, or have sex. All of these can be great things to do, but if they are done without God also working in our hearts and people witnessing those changes, then we are like the Pharisees.)

Have your students record their

answers on the labels and stick them to their water bottles.

Ask: **"Why do we try to hide behind our "labels"?** (It would be much less work to just cut the label off and let people see what is on the inside instead of trying to hide or maintain a charade. We should keep our hearts pure and let those around us see Jesus and what He is doing in our lives. God is more concerned about what is on the inside (a pure heart), rather than the outside (our "labels").

In Closing
Share with your D-Team that allowing God to work in an area of our lives and allowing those around us to see that work and be affected in a spiritual way is the real meaning of mission. We should stop working so hard to hide behind the labels in our lives.

To close the D-Team, encourage each student to make a commitment to give 100 percent to completing his or her personal mission. Point out that in the process, those around them (particularly the people they wrote down on their Mission Cards) will witness the changes in their lives and be drawn closer to Christ. If a student chooses to make this commitment, give him or her an opportunity to cut off the labels on his or her bottle and then read aloud the mission statement. Then ask one student to pray for that student immediately. Continue until all students have cut off their labels, read their mission statements, and been prayed for.

Take a break, stretch, and then come together again right after this D-Team to prepare for the Concert of Prayer. Remind students to fill and bring their water bottles to the Concert of Prayer.

Saturday Evening Activity–
Concert of Prayer

Preparation for Concert of Prayer and Communion

Explain to your students that you would like for them to spend a little time together preparing for communion before going into the Concert of Prayer. Ask your students to take out their water bottles and open them. Then read 1 John 1:7–9 aloud to your students.

Encourage your students to take the next few minutes as a time of private confession. If you have non-Christians in the group, don't exclude them. This is a great opportunity to share what it means to have a personal relationship with Christ. Ask if they would like to join in this time. Be sure to explain that communion is for believers and that it wouldn't be appropriate at this time to participate in the actual communion. Ask them if they would like to accept Christ as Lord at this time. Then let your students decide what to do.

Confession

Instruct your students to take off their shoes and socks and to think through the unconfessed sin in their lives that their feet play a role in carrying out. For instance, if there are places that they shouldn't have gone (party, movie, drinking, a date's bedroom, etc.), ask them to confess any past sins and ask God for forgiveness. Tell them, when they are ready, to pour a couple of drops of water on their feet as a symbol of asking for forgiveness and claiming the cleansing according to 1 John 1:9.

Continue with the hands. Ask your students to think through the unconfessed sin in their lives that their hands play a role in carrying out. For instance, if

they cheated, wrote a cruel letter, or hit someone, ask them to confess the sin and to ask for forgiveness. Tell them to pour a couple of drops of water on their hands as a symbol of asking for forgiveness and claiming the cleansing according to 1 John 1:9.

Continue with the lips and tongue. If they have said hurtful things to or about people, gossiped, or taken God's name in vain, ask them to confess the sin and to ask for forgiveness. Tell them to pour a couple of drops of water on their lips and tongue as a symbol of asking for forgiveness and claiming the cleansing according to 1 John 1:9.

Continue with the secret sins of the heart that no one else can see, but we know what they are. Ask your students to confess any sin and ask for forgiveness. Instruct your students to take a long drink of the water as a symbol of asking for forgiveness and claiming the cleansing according to 1 John 1:9.

Close the time together with prayer. Then go to the Concert of Prayer. Ask students to bring their Mission Cards.

Evening Activity– Concert of Prayer

This Concert of Prayer follows a D-Team in which students identified their unique mission from God. They also spent time "cleansing" their feet, hands, lips and tongue, and hearts symbolically with water. Their focus is already on God and His willingness to forgive sins. Use this time to continue worshiping God through prayer, Scripture reading, music, and communion.

Ask your students to stand in response to the area they need the most

Saturday Evening Activity–(cont.)
Concert of Prayer

help in fulfilling their personal missions. As you focus on the following areas, read aloud each of the corresponding Scriptures: accountability (Ecclesiastes 4:9–10); courage (1 Corinthians 16:13–14); discipline (1 Corinthians 9:26–27); faith (Hebrews 11:1); and self-control (Proverbs 25:28). As students stand, have a leader pray for them.

To set up communion, read 1 John 1:9 aloud. Explain that we are all sinners and we all need help in battling the sin in our lives. Ask everyone to stand up as you ask God for forgiveness and for help in overcoming sin.

Sing or play a song such as "Go and Sin No More" by Rebecca St. James *(God,* ForeFront, 1996) to close the Concert of Prayer.

SUNDAY

Schedule

7:00 AM	Mission #2
7:45 AM	Leaders' Meeting
8:00 AM	Breakfast
9:00 AM	Morning Session—**A Mission with Power**
10:30 AM	Pack to leave/Load buses
11:00 AM	Team Time
12:00 PM	Lunch
1:00 PM	Depart
5:00 PM	Arrive back at church

Mission #2

Mission #2 gives students an opportunity to continue building community with others from their campus team or small group. Give each campus team or small group a copy of Student Notes #4–Mission #2.

To complete CODE: 8.23.96.1A, possible answers might include: John 5:30; Ecclesiastes 3:1; Jeremiah 1:5–10; Matthew 28:16–20; James 1:5; Matthew 22:35–39.

To crack the second code, your students will need to think about the phrases, "tie a yellow ribbon around the old oak **tree**"; "**tree** of knowledge"; "And he will be like a **tree** firmly planted by streams of water" (Psalm 1:3); barking up the wrong **tree**; and weeping willow (a kind of **tree**). Teams should bring back a leaf, a piece of bark, or a small branch as evidence that they understood the clues.

To get the agent's signature, students should show up at the softball field (hopefully, you have one at your campsite) at home plate. A leader or leaders should be stationed there to explain the rest of the mission and to make sure teams complete it correctly. You can have several teams doing this at the same time. The mission is the ever-popular bat spin. Each team member must hold the bat upright on the ground and place his or her forehead on the top of the bat handle. After spinning around 20 times, he or she must run to first base (if there is a line-up, send another team running to third base). Students will be very dizzy after spinning and it will be a challenge to run a straight line. After a team is finished, they must run back to mission headquarters and turn in their list.

As teams show up at mission headquarters, check the answers on their lists and keep track of which team was the fastest and most accurate. Award a prize to the winning team.

Sunday
Morning Session

Program Cue Sheet

TIME	PROGRAM ELEMENT
8:45 AM	**DOORS OPEN/WALK-IN** Play some "high-energy" Christian music.
9:00 AM	**SONG** Have a vocalist sing, or play a CD of a song about God's power.
9:04 AM	**WORSHIP** Worship leader conducts 15 minutes of worship choruses.
9:19 AM	**MESSAGE—** **A MISSION WITH POWER** See Sunday Morning Message rationale and outline.
9:49 AM	**WORSHIP** Worship leader conducts 20 minutes of songs that focus on what was taught in the message.
10:10 AM	**ANNOUNCEMENTS AND DISMISS** Your host should pray, give directions for packing and loading buses, and announce where teams are meeting for team time.

Sunday Morning Message–
A Mission with Power

Big Idea

People love power and try various means to attain it. Power is an attractive commodity. Students will learn that the Gospel is an amazing source of power that can change the world. (Scriptural basis: Romans 1:16; 2 Peter 1:3–4; John 3:16; Romans 3:23; 6:23; 10:13; Titus 3:5)

As this series of messages concludes, lead the students to a definite planned action step as a result of understanding their mission. For example, sharing their faith with a friend is the one mission all students can take away from the retreat. In this session, the power of the Gospel will be shared and seeker students will have an opportunity to accept Christ as Lord and Savior.

Rationale

We can learn more about power if we understand three truths:
1. The world is searching for power.
2. There are different kinds of power.
3. The Good News of Jesus Christ is the ultimate power.

Message Outline

I. Introduction
    Think about people who possess power: bodybuilders have physical power; financial tycoons own monetary power; Hollywood actresses and actors often have sexual power; and political figures hold governmental power. Power is attractive to people.

II. The world is searching for power.
    a. Power is popular.
    b. Students are attracted to power. In school, the guy with the washboard stomach or the cool sports car, the athlete, or the cheerleader represent those who have power.

III. There are different kinds of power.
    a. Secular power.
    b. The power of God–real power! Read 2 Peter 1:3–4.

IV. The Gospel (Good News of Jesus Christ) is the ultimate power.
    a. Those who accept the Gospel receive power.
        • The power of the Gospel has literally changed the world. Illustration: Sharing the life-changing message of Christ with the lost is like dynamite blowing away the sinful person. When the dust clears, a new creation in God is standing amid the rubble.
    b. Those who have this power are not ashamed of the Gospel. Read Romans 1:16.
    c. Let us use this power of the Gospel and change the world!

V. Conclusion
    Share God's plan of salvation (Read John 3:16; Romans 3:23; 6:23; 10:13; Titus 3:5). Challenge students to make a personal commitment to Christ if they have not yet done so. Explain that purpose can never be actualized without the presence of Christ who speaks to us and gives us purpose. Close with a prayer of agreement and commitment that students will share the message of Christ individually and corporately. Celebrate the fact that their friends and family are about to hear the greatest news they have ever heard!

Retreat Follow-up

- Show pictures or video highlights of the retreat at your next student program.
- Follow up on new students who came to the retreat and make sure they stay connected in the ministry.
- Follow up immediately on students who made decisions to trust Christ.
- Use the momentum generated at the retreat and keep building on it by meeting together on a regular basis.
- Continue teaching topics related to what was taught at the retreat and casting the ministry vision.
- Encourage leaders to continue building relationships with the students in their small groups and to check on areas in which students committed to grow, especially what was written on their Mission Cards.
- About four weeks after the retreat, send students a "Mission Possible" card reminding them that with God, all things are possible. Give them directions to a special party at which you can encourage them to keep pursuing their missions. Ask students to share stories about their missions in front of the group and celebrate the ways God is at work in the hearts of these students and the friends on their Mission Cards.
- Provide opportunities for students to maintain the bonds they built by implementing or continuing a small group ministry and placing students on campus teams.
- Evaluate the retreat by asking the following questions:
  Did the facility serve us well? Would we go there again?
  Did we promote the retreat far enough in advance?
  How did students respond to the speaker? Would we ask him or her to speak at next year's retreat?
  Did the programming elements flow together smoothly?
  How did we do financially? Do we need to budget more money next year?
  Was the schedule too packed or was there the right amount of free time?
  Did we have the right leaders and enough volunteers to help?
  What did we learn?
  How can next year's retreat be better?
- Write thank-you notes to your leaders, speaker, and musicians.
- Call or write the campsite and thank the personnel for their help in making your retreat run smoothly.
- Take time to celebrate with your staff and/or leadership team the amazing things God did at the retreat.
- Rest!

Student Notes # 1
Mission # 1

Your mission, should you choose to accept it, is to complete this list and return it to mission headquarters. This is a race against the clock and other teams. You and your team must obtain the information required to complete this list. Covert agents will attempt to secure your information, so be careful! Remember, your information is **TOP SECRET!** Any misappropriation of Mission information will result in your termination from this mission. Should you or any of your team fail to comply with regulations, the mission director will disavow you and your team. You have one hour to complete your mission. Good luck!

1. From mission headquarters, you must take your selected team and meet at the rendezvous point. Your rendezvous point will be established by your mode of **transport**. Your **drive** will move you forward. Once you and your team secure the **model** and **make**, you will be responsible to document your findings below. Use this code and write down the information:

    CODE: 8.22.96.1A _____

2. Your transport has been established, so now take the high road to the **centers** where all agents reside. These headquarters have been given code names. You and your team must document all the **resident** code names and numeric date built, if available. Use this code and write down the information:

    CODE: 8.22.96.2A _____

3. Your list is now close to completion. You must find the place where **recreation** happens. When your team finds it, don't **play** around, but quickly assemble your team and start the search. Use your skills to determine what is required of you. It should involve a ball. Bring back proof of your mission and report to mission headquarters. Use this code and write down what kind of proof you are bringing:

    CODE: 8.22.96.3A _____

Student Notes #2
Be Still and Know

Read 1 Kings 19:9–13 and answer the following questions. Earlier in this chapter, we learn that the prophet Elijah's life had been threatened and he had escaped into the desert. He may have been facing a crisis of faith, identity, or vision. After being sustained by the angel of the Lord, Elijah journeyed to Mt. Horeb. Now, let's take a look at how God appeared to Elijah.

Where did God find Elijah?

Why do you think God asked Elijah, "What are you doing here?"

How did Elijah answer God's question?

How did God respond to Elijah's complaints that his work was fruitless?

After hearing God's invitation, what would you expect to happen next?

If you were standing there with Elijah and the wind came and tore up the mountain, would you naturally assume it was God trying to get your attention? Or if that didn't move you, what about the earthquake or fire?

After all that commotion, would you even pay attention to the whisper?

Why do you think God did not present Himself to Elijah in the wind, earthquake, and fire?

Reflection
Take the next 20–25 minutes to read the following meditation (adapted from Henri J. M. Nouwen's *Making All Things New: An Invitation to the Spiritual Life* [HarperCollins, 1981] and then be quiet.

Without solitude it is virtually impossible for us to live a spiritual life. Solitude begins with a time and a place for God alone. If we really believe not only that God exists but also that He is actively present in our lives–healing, teaching, and guiding–we need to set aside a time and a space to give Him our undivided attention.

Jesus says, "Go to your private room and, when you have shut your door, pray to the Father who is in that secret place" (Matthew 6:6, JB).

Even though bringing some solitude into our lives is one of the most necessary disciplines, it is also one of the most difficult disciplines. We may have a deep desire for real solitude, but as we try to enter into solitude there is a part of us that feels like we can't be completely alone and quiet for some unexplainable reason. Nouwen goes on to say that when we finally are alone–without friends, TV, or phones to distract us–an inner chaos opens within us.

This chaos can be so disturbing that we are anxious to get busy again. Going into a private room and shutting the door does not mean that we immediately shut out all our inner and outer distractions.

Outer distractions would be like the homework that has to be done, the shopping trip that is coming up, the get-together next weekend, and so forth. Inner distractions would include such thoughts about doubts, anxieties, fears, bad memories, unresolved conflicts, angry feelings, impulsive desires, bad habits, reoccurring sin, lack of discipline in an area of your life, a family issue, and so on.

On the contrary, when we have removed our outer distractions ("winds and earthquakes"), we often find that our inner distractions (mentioned above) show themselves to us in full force.

Don't run from inner and outer distractions. Ask yourself, *What are the "earthquakes" in my life?* As they pop into your head, record them in the space provided and then give them to Jesus through prayer. Ask Him to carry the burden of those distractions at least for the weekend. Then be silent again. God tells us to "be still, and know that I am God" (Psalm 46:10). Try to clear your mind of all the "earthquakes" so that you are able to hear the gentle voice of God.

Now, what are the inner distractions that need more attention? What is God trying to work on in your life? Record them below.

Hang on to your list of distractions and be prepared to take it back to the D-Team to share and work through together.

Student Notes #3
Reflection

I will _____

The first part of this mission statement is personal and lines up with the commandment to "love the Lord your God with all your heart and with all your soul and with all your mind" (Matthew 22:37). What part of your life is not reflecting this commandment?

Where are you not loving Him? In your heart? Soul? Mind?

What area of your life did God address during your solitude walk this morning?

So that I can bring _____ closer to Christ.

This second part of the statement lines up with the second commandment where Jesus says "love your neighbor as yourself." Who is the "neighbor" that will be affected by the changes that you wrote down in the first part of the mission statement?

For example, if prayer is an area in your life where you are not showing God that you love Him with your whole heart and mind, you might complete the statement in the following way:

I will commit to praying 30 minutes each morning so that I can bring my younger sisters closer to Christ.

Student Notes #4
Mission #2

The mission director was impressed with your ability to secure TOP SECRET information in Mission #1. He has decided to send you and your team out on another important, classified mission. Your mission, should you choose to accept it, is to again complete this list and the required covert activities. Your team will need at least one Bible for this mission. Should you or your team fail to comply with regulations, the mission director will disavow you and your team and send you to Siberia for 30 years of hard labor. You have one hour to complete your mission. Again, good luck!

1. Agent Ethan Hunt needs your help! He does not know any Bible verses on the subject of discovering and knowing your God-given mission. Can you help him? In the space below, write out three Bible verses that might help him understand what mission is all about and use this code:

    CODE: 8.23.96.1A

2. The following random words and sayings mysteriously appeared at mission headquarters. Your team must determine what it all means and where it might lead you. Bring back some kind of evidence that you cracked the code.

                  tie a yellow ribbon

                                              Psalm 1:3

knowledge

                       barking   weeping

3. The list is almost complete, but you must hurry! For those of you who are missing **home**, go here for further instructions. Have the assigned agent sign below to verify the completion of this mission:

         Agent signature_____

PWR

Retreat Summary: This camp focuses on the power of the Holy Spirit in a Christian's life. Students will be challenged to **P**ray, **W**itness, and **R**ely on Him (PWR) as they reach out to their non-Christian friends and share their faith.

Length of Retreat: Friday night through Sunday afternoon.

Target Audience: Christian students, but non-Christians will learn that the power source is available to them if they trust in Christ.

Facility Requirements: A hotel or retreat center large enough to accommodate your group.

Retreat Objectives:
- To teach students that the Holy Spirit is the power source of a Christian's life.
- To show students the power of community.
- To give students opportunities to build relationships with one another.
- To build memories.
- To challenge students to pray, witness, and rely on God.

Introduction: People try many things to feel powerful. Those in the business world wear power ties and arrange power lunches in hopes of impressing clients and increasing the company's bottom line. When successful, they go on power trips, impressing even themselves. Military officers power up and use their rank to mistreat or patronize their platoons. Athletes eat power bars to give them energy for peak performance, and they lift weights to build their muscles.

Over time, people learn that power can be fleeting–some days you may feel strong and powerful, but on other days, you feel weak and helpless. As Christians, we do not need to strive and search for power. We have a constant source of power to fuel our lives–the power of God. He has given us the Holy Spirit to guide and assist us in life. This weekend retreat is designed to teach students about the Holy Spirit and to equip them with the necessary tools to take advantage of the power that God offers to every believer. Students will be challenged to **P**ray, **W**itness, and **R**ely on Him (PWR) as they reach out to their non-Christian friends and share their faith.

Retreat Checklist

ACTIVITIES
___ Movie or video
___ Elements for communion

COMPETITION
___ Soccer balls
___ Footballs
___ Sleds
___ Equipment for video tournament
___ Frisbee and cones for Ultimate Frisbee

D-TEAMS
___ Crayons and paper
___ Size "A" battery, lightbulb, and 6" gauge copper wire
___ Butcher paper
___ Ball of yarn
___ Prayer checks

EMERGENCIES
___ First Aid Kit
___ Names and phone numbers of each camper's parent or guardian
___ Name and directions to nearest hospital from campsite

HANDOUTS AND SUPPLIES
___ Student notebook
___ Student Notes #1, #2, and #3
___ Leader Responsibility Sheets
___ Extra Bibles
___ Camera and/or video

PROGRAMS
___ Musical instruments
___ Props for stage
___ Video of a rocket blasting off
___ Walk-in music as students enter program
___ Song sheets or slides for worship choruses
___ Yearbooks, calendar, and cross (Sunday morning message)

REGISTRATION
___ Completed permission slips from each camper and leader
___ Room assignments
___ Petty cash box to collect remaining payments for camp

VEHICLES
___ Maps to campsite
___ Insurance documents
___ Money for gas and tolls

This is a sample letter we gave to all D-Team leaders at a meeting prior to camp. Along with this letter, leaders also received D-Team material to study and prepare.

Dear D-Team Leader:

After many weeks of prayer, preparation, and trying to get your students to turn in their registration forms, PWR is almost here. As you think about this weekend, you probably feel a sense of anticipation as well as nervousness. Take a deep breath and relax–you don't have to do this weekend on your own. You have access to a *great* power source. Relying on the Holy Spirit is the most important thing you can do in preparation for PWR.

During the weekend, your students will hear about the power of the Holy Spirit, the Word, prayer, and community. Before you try to lead and care for your students, make sure that you set aside time this week to listen to God and plug in to these power sources. Read the book of Acts and see for yourself the awesome power of our God. Also, pray that

- the students who have not yet accepted Christ will come to know Him this weekend.
- the students who are not yet in D-Teams will feel accepted and have a desire to be in a D-Team.
- the students will begin to understand God's power and take steps to rely on Him.
- the message givers will communicate God's Word clearly and will be empowered by Him.
- there will be safety in travel.
- our ministry will receive protection.
- our leaders will have direction, discernment, and strength.

During PWR, you will have the privilege of leading your students in their D-Teams and allowing them to experience God's power firsthand. Your D-Team will sit together during mealtimes, the four main sessions, and at the Concert of Prayer. Because you will be together during these sessions, you will have the opportunity to be creative and "own" your meeting area by decorating it and bringing notes or gifts to your students each session.

The sessions are designed to be interactive so that you will also have opportunities to lead discussions or activities with your D-Team. The D-Team material will give you all the information and ideas you will need to lead your D-Team throughout the weekend. There are also leadership meetings scheduled each day. The following checklist will help you remember your main responsibilities for each session:

- Be prepared spiritually. Set aside time to pray and listen to God.
- Bring something to decorate your meeting area for each session. Possible ideas: personal notes, candy, gum, vitamins, power bars, toys, pictures, etc. Be creative!
- Study the D-Team curriculum.

Thank you for your commitment and passion to see high school students grow into fully devoted followers of Christ. Your role is the cornerstone of this weekend and is greatly valued and appreciated. It will be exciting to come together after this weekend and see how God's power worked through you!

Retreat Overview

Theme
This weekend retreat is based on the theme of power and the Holy Spirit. Student Impact created a lightning bolt retreat logo and used it on the retreat brochure, T-shirts, and handouts.

Handouts
Every student should be given some kind of handout or notebook to use for taking notes or journaling. You may want to include your retreat schedule in this handout as well as camp rules, a camp map, and information on various issues. Encourage students to bring their notebooks to all sessions and D-Teams. For this retreat, Student Impact created a booklet with the retreat logo on the front and blank pages for notes.

Take-Away
Consider giving each student some kind of tangible reminder of their camp experience. A take-away object plays an important part in reminding students of their time at camp and how God worked. A possible idea for a take-away for this camp is giving students keychain flashlights (a source of power) with the retreat name (PWR) screened on them to help students remember to pray, witness, and rely. Student Impact ordered these keychains from a corporate gift catalog and built the cost into the retreat fee.

Schedule
A sample daily schedule used by Student Impact for PWR is included as a guideline to help you develop your own schedule. While schedules can be restrictive at times, they will keep your leaders and students organized each day and help make your time together purposeful.

Quiet Times
On the two mornings of this retreat, your students will have the opportunity to encounter God in quiet times. These quiet times will help your students focus on specific Scripture passages. If a student isn't in the habit of meeting with God on a daily basis, a quiet time may motivate him or her to develop a routine of reading the Bible and praying daily. Encourage your leaders to use this time to assist any young believers who may be trying to do a quiet time for the first time.

Competition
Brainstorm with your leadership team a competitive activity that all your students will enjoy. It's fun to offer some kind of competition that requires scoring points, so that you can announce a winning team.

Here are some suggestions for competition:
- Snow, mud, or rain makes a great field for soccer or football games.
- If you have snow and a hill, a sledding contest for distance is always a winner.
- A video game tournament would fit the power theme. Set up Nintendo stations and organize students into teams. See which team can score the highest points.
- Ultimate Frisbee tournament—the object of Ultimate Frisbee is to pass the Frisbee from teammate to teammate in order to move it up the field

and score in the end zone. The only equipment you need is a Frisbee and a few cones to mark off the field. Here's how to play:

Start the game by having one team "kick off" by throwing the Frisbee from their end zone. Two rules apply to the offensive team: they must throw the Frisbee, not hand it off; and they may not take more than three steps while in possession of the Frisbee. One major rule applies to the defensive team: they may only have one person guard the offensive player in possession of the Frisbee. Possession of the Frisbee changes whenever the Frisbee hits the ground, is intercepted, or is thrown out of bounds. At that time, the defensive team takes over from the point where the Frisbee hit the ground or where it broke the plane of the out-of-bounds line. After a team scores by throwing the Frisbee into the end zone, award one point to the offensive team and have them "kick off" to start play again.

D-Teams

D-Teams (small groups) give students a chance to discuss and apply what they are learning. It might be helpful to send a letter a week before the retreat to all the D-Team leaders and encourage them to prepare for this retreat. A sample of the letter used by Student Impact can be found on page 152. The following descriptions give an overview of the D-Teams for the weekend:

D-Team #1–Plugging In
During this D-Team, students will have a chance to get to know each other better, which will allow the next level of vulnerability to take place.

D-Team #2–The Power Source
The goal of this D-Team is to help students better understand the Holy Spirit as a power source for Christians.

D-Team #3–Power Line
In this D-Team, students will draw timelines of their lives to see how they have been influenced by the Holy Spirit.

D-Team #4–The Power of Community
During this D-Team, students will discover their personal importance to the D-Team community.

D-Team #5–The Power of Commitment
In this D-Team, students will discover how journaling or writing out their prayers can help them be more consistent in their prayer lives.

Programs

All programming elements are designed to move each student emotionally and intellectually to see God's love by exposing God's truth in a relevant, practical way through the communicative arts. Each program points students toward a basic biblical truth. Sample Cue Sheets include suggested program orders.

Here are a few ideas, materials, and props you may want to use in planning your programs:

Ideas
1.   Place a large video screen at the front of your meeting area. Run some sort of video or show slides depicting electricity and energy. Find a video showing lightning, power surges, or forms of energy, such as *Phenomenon*. If using slides, make the graphics look electrical by using lightning bolts, power lines, or lightbulbs.
2.   Because D-Teams happen during the messages, arrange for students and

leaders to sit around tables.

3. Place atomic symbols made into models as centerpieces for the tables. Or place a power granola bar or bottle of vitamins on each table.

4. Use sound effects found on CDs, like thunder, electrical currents, or rockets blasting, as students walk into or exit the program.

Materials/Props

To make the stage fit the power theme, hang wires or cable from the ceiling. Cut lightning bolts out of cardboard or foam core to use as stage props. Use strobe lights as students are walking into the program.

Messages

Four messages are included in this retreat. This retreat is unique because the D-Teams are integrated into the programs and messages. This interactive approach will add variety to your programs. You need to carefully study the D-Teams so that you can effectively teach the topic by using the D-Teams to build on your messages. Use the material provided, but take time to hear what the Holy Spirit wants to communicate to your students through you.

Student Impact's speaker for this retreat was Dan Webster, the former Executive Director of Student Impact at Willow Creek Community Church. Dan currently is the president of Authentic Leadership, an organization dedicated to teaching and training men and women to be authentic as they lead others.

Here are brief summaries of the evening and morning messages:

Friday Evening Message–Power of the Holy Spirit

This message gives biblical teaching on the Holy Spirit's role in our lives and in the lives of our friends.

Saturday Morning Message–Power of Teamwork

Many students have a limited understanding of biblical community and the power of working together. This message will assist students in learning about this concept on a deeper level by looking at God's Word and what He says about its value.

Saturday Evening Message–PWR Play

This is the key message of the retreat. Students will be motivated to reach out to their friends by praying for them, witnessing to them by telling their story and living lives of integrity, and relying on the Holy Spirit to work in their friends' lives.

Sunday Morning Message–Power in Action

In this message, you will lay out your ministry's plan for evangelism when students return home. This message requires the following props: a yearbook from each high school represented in your ministry; a large six-month calendar; and a cross. You also need to preprint prayer cards (see page 173) to give each student at the end of the message.

Evening Activities

For each day, we list a suggested evening activity. Plan to do a cabin check each night and make sure that each student is in his or her cabin. You can expect high school students to pull pranks like cabin raids even after "lights out." Think about how you and your team will handle these kinds of issues before the camp begins.

Friday

Schedule

6:00 PM	Registration
7:00 PM	Leaders' Meeting
8:00 PM	Evening Session– **Power of the Holy Spirit** D-Team #1– **Plugging In** D-Team #2– **The Power Source**
9:45 PM	D-Team #3– **Power Line**
11:00 PM	Movie and Popcorn
1:00 AM	Lights Out

Friday
Evening Session

Program Cue Sheet

TIME	PROGRAM ELEMENT
7:45 PM	**DOORS OPEN/WALK-IN** Play some "high-energy" Christian music.
8:00 PM	**VIDEO** Show a video of a rocket blastoff with high-energy music accompanying it.
8:03 PM	**SONG** Have a vocalist sing, or play a CD of a song focused on God's power.
8:07 PM	**WELCOME/ ANNOUNCEMENTS** Host should welcome every one and explain the retreat rules: • Be at all **m**eals. • Be at all **m**eetings. • Be **m**odest in all you do and say.
8:12 PM	**WORSHIP** Worship leader selects four or five "up-tempo" celebrative songs to kick off the weekend. (See Appendix C for a list of choruses.)
8:25 PM	**D-TEAM #1– PLUGGING IN** D-Team leaders facilitate discussion around their tables based on D-Team #1 material.
8:40 PM	**VIDEO–D-TEAM POWER** Show a video of several students giving testimonies of their experiences in their D-Teams. If you are unable to shoot the video before the retreat, have the students share their stories "live."
8:44 PM	**TOPIC INTRODUCTION** Host introduces retreat theme, gives brief overview of tonight's message on the Holy Spirit, and instructs leaders to begin D-Team #2.
8:49 PM	**D-TEAM #2– THE POWER SOURCE** D-Team leaders facilitate discussion around their tables based on D-Team #2 material.
9:10 PM	**MESSAGE– POWER OF THE HOLY SPIRIT** See Friday Evening Message rationale and outline.
9:40 PM	**ANNOUNCEMENTS AND DISMISSAL** Host prays, gives the schedule for Saturday, and dismisses students to D-Team #3.

D-Team #1 –
Plugging In

Objective

By now your students will have checked into their rooms, figured out where all the strategic persons of the opposite sex are rooming, and made plans for late-night raids. In other words, they are excited to be here. Your challenge will be to help them focus that energy on this first D-Team experience so they can learn about the Holy Spirit.

Since this is the first time your D-Team will be together for the weekend, plan something to create a real sense of "ownership" in your group. Bring crayons so they can autograph their spot at the table. Decorate the table (you can sit at the same table for the rest of the weekend) according to the retreat theme of power.

Write each student in your group letters telling them what you hope they accomplish this weekend. After your students participate in this session, they should begin to break down relational barriers with other students in your D-Team and start to form bonds.

Materials Needed

- Crayons
- Paper

Get to Know Each Other

Give your students some time to catch up with each other and establish relationships. Try to create the feeling that your D-Team is a safe place where students can be honest by asking the following questions:

- **Can we set a goal as a group for how many hours of sleep we will get this weekend?**
- **What do you like most about our ministry? Why?**
- **Why did you decide to come to this retreat?**
- **What is the one thing that you hope happens this weekend more than anything else?**

D-Team #2–
The Power Source

Objective
Most students are familiar with two-thirds of the Trinity: God the Father and Jesus Christ who died for our sins, but they may be unclear on the Holy Spirit's role. After your students participate in this session, they should have a better understanding of the Holy Spirit as a power source for Christians.

Materials Needed
- Bibles
- 1 "A" battery, lightbulb, and 6" gauge of copper wire

Holy Spirit Experiment
Read aloud Acts 4:1–7. Explain to your students that Peter and John were preaching about the resurrection when they were arrested. Say, **"The rulers, elders, and teachers of the law wanted to know how Peter was able to heal a cripple."** Read aloud Acts 4:8, emphasizing the fact that Peter was filled with the Holy Spirit. Say, **"In the same way, we want to discover more about how we can be filled with the power promised through the Holy Spirit."**

Touch one end of the wire to the bottom of the battery and touch the light bulb to the top of the battery with the other end of the wire touching it on its side. Allow a few minutes for students to try this and note the results.

Explain that the Holy Spirit plays a role in our lives similar to the wires: He "conducts" God's power to us if Christ is the battery of our lives. Ask,

- **What do you think it means to let the Holy Spirit "conduct" God's power in your life?**
- **When have you heard the Holy Spirit speaking to you?**
- **What keeps you from hearing the Holy Spirit?**
- **How can the Holy Spirit help you today? When you go back to school?**

The message will continue after this D-Team so the speaker will explain how this concept can be applied to daily life.

In Closing
Ask one of your students to thank God for the Holy Spirit and to pray that each person will regularly plug into the power source.

Big Idea

Students rarely have a clear understanding or confidence in the reality of the Holy Spirit's work in their lives or in their friends' lives. This message will give biblical background for the Holy Spirit's role in a Christian's life.

Rationale

Each student can have more confidence in God's work by remembering some simple facts about the power and work of the Holy Spirit.

Message Outline

I. The power of the Holy Spirit was involved in our conversion–every Christian's life has a supernatural beginning.

   a. God draws people to Jesus Christ– it's how every Christian comes to faith. Read John 6:44 and then take a few moments to allow students to reflect on the circumstances around their conversions. Ask them to look for signs of God's involvement, such as inner restlessness, a friend being moved to share with them, a praying relative, etc. Say, **"Whether the Holy Spirit drew you to Jesus Christ through circumstances or friends, remember: it was God at work!"**

   b. It is the Holy Spirit, not you, who will draw your friends to faith in Jesus Christ. Read John 16:7–8. Jesus even reminded His disciples of this truth!

II. The Holy Spirit was the power behind the beginning of the New Testament church.

   a. Read Acts 4:31–33 and ask your students, **"What is the power source of the New Testament church?"**

   b. The apostle Peter was empowered and inspired by the Holy Spirit to preach a message that resulted in 3,000 people becoming Christians. Read Acts 2:4, 14, 22, 37–41 and emphasize the presence and power of the Holy Spirit in conversions. The Holy Spirit births and builds the church through His power, not our power.

   c. Jesus reminded His disciples of this truth. Reread John 16:7–8 and point out the Holy Spirit's convicting power.

III. The key to experiencing God's power is to be continually filled with the Holy Spirit.

   a. Read Ephesians 5:18 and point out the following three truths about the filling of the Holy Spirit:

   • "Be filled" is a present, continuous verb tense. For example, breathing is something we must continually do to experience life. Being filled with the Holy Spirit on an ongoing basis is what we need to experience God's life.

   • The Holy Spirit comes to those who by faith yield and surrender their lives to Christ.

   • The Holy Spirit comes to those who ask.

IV. Application
   a. Invite students to thank God for His involvement in their conversion.
   b. Invite students to thank God for His involvement in starting the New Testament church.
   c. Invite students to ask God to fill them with the Holy Spirit by faith as they surrender their lives to His control and power. Ask students to stand if they are willing to pray this prayer and then lead them in a prayer.

D-Team #3–
Power Line

Objective
During this D-Team, your students will draw timelines of their lives to see how they have been influenced by the Holy Spirit.

Materials Needed
- Bibles
- Long roll of butcher paper, crayons

Real Power
Explain to your students that the book of Acts is probably one of the most exciting books in the Bible because it is packed with incredible stories from the early years of the church. Say, **"Over and over again, Luke tells us about people who witnessed the power of the Holy Spirit, the Word, prayer, worship, and community. It is amazing to look at the timeline of events in Acts and see how many times God revealed His power to His people."**

Ask a student to read aloud Acts 16:22–34 to get a taste of God's power. Emphasize that God's power did not stop with the early church. Say, **"We still witness the power of the Holy Spirit and are changed by it today. Let's take a look at the 'Power Line' of your own lives to see how God has made His power real to you."**

Allow about 10 minutes for your students to draw timelines of their lives on butcher paper. Encourage them to draw or illustrate all the major events that have occurred in their lives. Instruct them to draw their line upward when good things happened and downward when they have gone through rough times.

After completing the timelines, have each person describe his or hers. It will be especially exciting to hear how God has led each person to your group. Ask the following questions: **"Where do you expect to see your timeline at the end of this weekend? How can we help you get there? How do you need to see the Holy Spirit's power in your life today?"**

In Closing
Take time to pray for each other. Have each student pray for the person on his or her left, asking the Holy Spirit to reveal His power this weekend. Distribute copies of Student Notes #1 and give your students instructions for their Saturday Morning Quiet Time.

Evening Activity–
Movie and Popcorn
We showed the movie *The Power of One*. After the movie, dismiss students to their rooms. Make sure you have a team of volunteers to check and see if students are staying in their assigned rooms. If needed, you might want to have a "hall patrol team" on duty in shifts throughout the night.

Saturday

Schedule

7:00 AM Quiet Time

8:00 AM Breakfast

8:30 AM Leaders' Meeting

9:15 AM Morning Session–
Power of Teamwork
D-Team #4–
Power of Community

10:30 AM D-Team #5–
The Power of Commitment

11:30 AM Competition

12:30 PM Lunch

1:30 PM One-on-Ones

2:00 PM Free Time

5:00 PM Dinner

6:00 PM Leaders' Meeting

7:00 PM Evening Session–
PWR Play

9:00 PM Preparation for Concert of Prayer

10:00 PM Concert of Prayer

12:00 AM Lights Out

Saturday
Morning Session

Program Cue Sheet

TIME	PROGRAM ELEMENT
8:30 AM	**LEADERS' MEETING** Led by Student Minister
9:00 AM	**DOORS OPEN/WALK-IN** Play some "high energy" Christian music.
9:15 AM	**VIDEO–ROCKET BLASTOFF** Use the same video of a rocket blastoff from Friday Evening Session.
9:16 AM	**SONG** Have a vocalist sing, or play a CD of a song about the power of community.
9:20 AM	**ANNOUNCEMENTS** Host should announce any pertinent information regarding the day's schedule.
9:25 AM	**WORSHIP** Worship leader selects six to eight worship choruses that connect to the theme of community.
9:50 AM	**MESSAGE– POWER OF TEAMWORK** See Saturday Morning Message rationale and outline.
10:20 AM	**D-TEAM #4– POWER OF COMMUNITY** D-Team leaders facilitate discussion around their tables based on D-Team #4 material.
10:30 AM	**PRAYER AND DISMISSAL** Host prays and dismisses students to D-Team #5.

Saturday Morning Message—
Power of Teamwork

Big Idea
Students benefit every day from the strength of doing things in teams. They win games as they play together on athletic teams; they earn money as they work together at their jobs; and they pass tests as they study together. Students need to see how working together can be a powerful way of reaching their friends for Christ.

Rationale
Every student can experience the power and benefits of reaching their friends for Christ by applying the five lessons of Mark 2:1–12.

I. Introduction
    Ask students to share what they believe to be the common characteristics of great sports teams throughout history. They may think of the Green Bay Packers or the Chicago Bulls or the New York Yankees. Record their answers on a flipchart or overhead projector.

II. Read Mark 2:1–12. There are five important lessons to learn from this passage.
    a. Lesson #1: The four friends formed a team to help a friend in need (Mark 2:1–3). Every student has friends who need to come to Christ. Who can they form a team with?
    b. Lesson #2: The friends had an objective (Mark 2:3). Their goal was to get their friend to Jesus.
    c. Lesson #3: The friends were creative (Mark 2:4). They literally tore the roof off the house to get

their friend to Jesus. It was not easy, but when they faced an obstacle they got creative. Nothing worth doing gets done easily. Make a list of creative ways to reach friends and record the answers on the flipchart or overhead projector.

    d. Lesson #4: The friends were determined (Mark 2:4). They did not quit at the first difficulty; they stayed with it until the job was done. Emphasize that the degree to which you love your friend determines how hard you will work. Refer to 1 Thessalonians 1 (love means hard work).
    e. Lesson #5: The friends were faith-filled (Mark 2:5). Jesus responded to the faith of the friends, not the faith of the paraplegic. They had confidence that Jesus could heal their friend! Ask, **"How much faith do you have that your friend will come to Christ?"**

III. Use one of the simulations listed below to illustrate the power and importance of teams.

Simulation #1: Rope-a-Dope
Suspend a rope between two poles about four feet off the ground and set the poles about six feet apart. Select two students to help you with this simulation. Ask a fairly large guy and a smaller guy to participate. Tell the smaller student that his task is to get his friend over the rope without his friend helping or touching the rope. He must be lifted over without touching the rope. The other side of the rope is symbolic of getting the friend

to Christ (the student receiving Jesus as Savior and Lord). After he discovers that he cannot do it, have him select as many friends as are needed to accomplish the task. Ask the students to talk about the power and importance of a team.

Simulation #2: The Table Lift

Ask two students to volunteer for a creative learning experience. Have one student sit on a table and ask the other student to attempt to lift and move the student to the other side of the room. Moving the student to the other side of the room is symbolic of a friend becoming a Christian. Be sure that you place the larger student on the table. Your students will have quite a laugh if you instruct the guy to sit on the table and have a smaller girl try to drag him across the room. When it becomes apparent that she cannot get the job done, allow her to select three friends to assist her in accomplishing the task. The four of them should be able to do together what she could not do alone. Have the students discuss the lessons learned from this simulation and then have them apply it to the task of evangelism.

IV. Application

Have students form teams of four and pray for three friends. Discuss how to creatively get the message of Christ to their friends.

D-Team #4–
Power of Community

Objective

During the previous sessions, your students heard how they can plug into the power of the Holy Spirit. Tonight they will have the opportunity to see what happens when we are one in Christ. During this session, your students will discover their importance to the D-Team community.

Materials Needed

- Bibles
- A ball of yarn

Community Builder

The object of this activity is to help your students understand each person's importance to your D-Team community. Take the ball of yarn, hold onto the end of the string, and toss the ball to one of your students. As the student catches it, say something that will encourage or affirm him or her. You might say something like, **"I'm glad you are here, because . . . "** or **"I appreciate you, because . . . "** or **"You are unique or important to our group, because . . ."** Then, have the student hold on to the string, toss the ball of yarn to someone else and say something to encourage or affirm him or her. Continue this process until everyone is holding on to the string and has been affirmed at least once. You will want to be prepared to say something for each person in the case no one else affirms a given student. If time allows, go around the circle more than once.

After everyone has had the chance to be affirmed, talk about the web of string that is now in the middle of your circle. Ask: **What does this web illustrate about community? What happens if one person leaves and drops his or her string? What would happen if you continued to toss the ball of yarn to each other in affirmation? What would happen if more people joined our circle?**

Read aloud Acts 2:42–47. As you look at these verses, ask, **"What does our D-Team need to do to experience the power of being in community?"**

In Closing

Tell your D-Team that each person is invited to be a member of the community that is described in these verses. Close this D-Team in prayer.

D-Team #5–
Power of Commitment

Objective
During this D-Team, your students will discover how journaling or writing down their prayers can help them be more consistent in their prayer lives.

Materials Needed
- Bibles
- An old prayer journal of your own
- A prayer check for each student

Hour of Prayer
Read aloud Acts 3:1. Say, **"The custom of early church believers was to go to the temple every day for an hour of prayer. Sounds like a pretty basic idea, doesn't it? Set aside a block of time each day to pray. No wonder the power of the Holy Spirit was so evident in the believers' lives. We could use a similar custom, couldn't we?"**

Ask a student to read aloud Acts 2:28. Explain that this verse is quoted from Psalm 16:8–11, which is just one of many great psalms of praise written by David to God. Say, **"David must have had an awesome journal. In this D-Team, you will experience writing out, or journaling, your prayers, in the form of a letter to God."**

Explain that prayer is simply communicating with God, and that today your students will be writing their prayers in a journal. Be prepared to share an old prayer journal of your own to let them see some examples of letters you have written to God. Encourage your students to look at some examples of letters that David wrote to God: Psalms 8, 25, 31, 61, 62. Emphasize that writing a letter to God should be no different or no more mysterious than writing a letter to your best friend.

Before you send your students off to write their letters, give each student a "prayer check" and tell them that while they are writing their letters to God, they should talk to him about committing to pray a certain amount of time each week. They can then write out a "prayer check" to God to make that commitment. Explain to them that they should make out the amount in hours.

Give your students 30 minutes to write their letters and fill out their prayer checks. Then meet back together to close the D-Team experience. Invite volunteers to share their letters, but give your students the right to keep their letters personal. Instruct your students to bring their prayer checks with them to the evening message.

In Closing
Take 10 minutes and pray for each student by name. Ask God to encourage and strengthen him or her to stick to the prayer commitment that he or she has made.

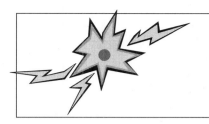

Saturday
Evening Session

Program Cue Sheet

TIME   **PROGRAM ELEMENT**

6:00 PM   **LEADERS' MEETING**
Led by Student Minister.

6:45 PM   **DOORS OPEN/WALK-IN**
Play some "high-energy" Christian music.

7:00 PM   **SONG**
Have a vocalist sing, or play a CD of a song focused on sharing Christ with others.

7:08 PM   **PWR PLAY INTRODUCTION**
Speaker or leader explains why we should have compassion for our non-Christian friends and defines the PWR Play. The PWR Play is to pray, witness, and rely on God as we share Him with friends.

7:38 PM   **D-TEAM TABLE DISCUSSION**
Speaker or leader asks D-Teams to discuss "Who has God given you compassion for and why?"

8:00 PM   **WORSHIP**
Worship leader should select worship choruses to fit the message topic of evangelism.

8:30 PM   **MESSAGE–PWR PLAY**
See Saturday Evening Message rationale and outline.

9:00 PM   **PRAYER AND DISMISSAL**
Instruct D-Team leaders to give students Student Notes #2–Letter from God. This letter personally invites students to a Concert of Prayer. Give students 30–45 minutes to read their letters and listen to what God has to say to them. Then ask students to bring their Letter from God and their prayer checks to the Concert of Prayer in one hour.

Saturday Evening Message–
PWR Play

Big Idea

This is the key message for the retreat. The goal of this message is to challenge students to step up and take the job of witnessing far more seriously. Help them see what they can and must do as they attempt to extend the love and message of Jesus Christ to their friends.

Rationale

Your students can be effective witnesses for Jesus Christ by doing the right things as they simply play their role in witnessing as defined by Paul in Colossians 4:2–6.

Message Outline

I. Read Colossians 4:2–6. Every student's role is to
a. Pray Right–"be devoted to prayer" (Colossians 4:2–4).
    • Discuss the word *devoted*. Determine what students are devoted to these days. Note that people give time, effort, and money to things that they are devoted to.
    • Prayer keeps us clear on who is in control. God is the One who is working in our friends' lives; it is His work (see 1 Corinthians 3:5–9; Paul reminds us that we are simply "fellow workers" and that God is the One who causes spiritual growth).
    • What does it look like to be devoted to prayer? Challenge your students to write the numbers "4:2" on their hands each morning for a week to remind them to pray.

b. Live Right–"conduct yourselves with wisdom toward outsiders" (Colossians 4:5).
    • Students know that they can do things that turn off their friends to the message of Christ. Have them put together a list of "bogus behaviors that blow our witness for Jesus." (They will probably say things like "be a hypocrite," "be selfish," "lie," or "cheat.")
    • Help students understand that it is not just "not doing" certain things that is important. Discuss with them the power of a loving attitude in laying the groundwork for the words we speak.

c. Talk Right–"let your words be gracious" (Colossians 4:6).
    • Knowing what to say and when to say it takes wisdom and experience. Remind students that you can say too much too soon or too little too late. Think of examples of each. We know what it is like to be assaulted by a well-meaning Christian with more truth than we are ready to hear, and we know what it is like to have a door wide open and not walk through it. Come up with illustrations of both.
    • Notice that our words are to be "gracious." What does *gracious* mean? (gentle, kind, and not obnoxious)

II. Have each student identify which of the above three roles they do well and which ones they do poorly. Then have them pray for each other in groups of four. You might use a self-evaluation tool such as the following:

Check where you are on the lines below:

	I'm Doing Poorly	I Need to Grow	I'm Doing Great
Pray Right	_____		
Living Right	_____		
Talking Right	_____		

Evening Activity– Concert of Prayer

After your students receive their Letter from God, use the next half hour to set up for the Concert of Prayer. Prepare the communion elements. Get the room set up. The Concert of Prayer should be a celebration and a reminder to students that without God, we are powerless. During the Concert of Prayer, spend some time praying, worshiping God, and celebrating communion. Lead your students in communion in a way that is appropriate for your church's theology and traditions.

Toward the end of the Concert of Prayer, challenge students to make a commitment to pray, witness, and rely on God. Ask students to write down the names of the friends they want to pray for and witness to. When they are ready, invite students to come forward and pin their piece of paper to the cross. Give students flashlight key chains with PWR screened on them which will remind them of their commitment and of the power they have through the Holy Spirit. Be sure to distribute copies of Student Notes #3–Sunday Morning Quiet Time to your students.

SUNDAY

Schedule

8:00 AM   Quiet Time

9:00 AM   Breakfast

9:30 AM   Leaders' Meeting

10:00 AM   Morning Session–
Power in Action

12:30 PM   Check Out

Sunday Morning Session Program Cue Sheet

TIME	PROGRAM ELEMENT
9:30 AM	**LEADERS' MEETING** Led by Student Minister.
10:00 AM	**DOORS OPEN/WALK-IN** Play some "high-energy" Christian music.
10:15 AM	**SONG** Have a vocalist sing, or play a CD of a song about evangelism.
10:20 AM	**MESSAGE–** **POWER IN ACTION** See Sunday Morning Message rationale and outline.
10:50 AM	**WORSHIP** Worship leader selects six to eight worship choruses which connect to the theme of evangelism.
11:15 AM	**CLOSING PRAYER** Take a few minutes to thank God for an incredible weekend together. Thank Him for the memories, new friendships, powerful teaching, and time with fellow D-Team members. Ask God to keep your group safe as they travel back home.

Sunday Morning Message–
Power in Action

Big Idea
In this session, you will share your ministry's plan for evangelism. Lay out three simple but strategic steps to make evangelism work in your ministry back home.

Rationale
Your student ministry will be effective in doing evangelism back home if everyone centers their thoughts and thinks on the right things.

Materials Needed
You will need three props to make this message work. Get a yearbook from each high school that your ministry draws from; a calendar for the following six months big enough for everyone to see; and a cross of some type that is visible to everyone.

Message Outline
I. To make evangelism happen back home, we must do three things:
    a. Think Faces.
        • Take evangelism from some abstract concept to the real faces of students on campus. Hold open a yearbook and show students the photos of their friends. Ask them if they have ever prayed for every student on their campus. Divide the students into prayer triplets and have them pray for a couple pages of photos and names.
        • Tell them that while you do not attend a high school campus, you do live in a neighborhood. Let them know what friends you are praying for each day. Describe the face of that person that you are going to share Christ with in the coming month. You cannot ask your stu-

dents to do something that you are not modeling.
    b. Think Dates.
        • Show students strategic times on the calendar over the next six months when you will devote prayer toward evangelism. Also show them when you will offer additional training addressing this topic. List evangelism conferences that you will attend as a group to keep motivated to do evangelism.
        • Have students think "real world" now. Ask them to think of their schedules in the coming week and how they can practically be witnesses for Christ to their friends. Have them list five ways they can be a witness for Christ in the coming week. Do not get hung up on verbally sharing; have them think of loving things they might do to express Christ's love to their friends.
    c. Think the Cross.
        • With the cross in the background, filled with the names of non-Christian friends, remind students that the Cross is why we share with our friends. Jesus' death calls us into action as we begin to lay our lives down for our friends.

II. Application.
    To close, give your students prayer cards that they can take home with them that will remind them to pray for three specific friends. You may want to preprint the cards with a statement at the top of the card saying something like, *Because Jesus died for me, I will pray every day for my friend to understand that Jesus died for him or her.*

Retreat Follow-up

- Show pictures or video highlights from the retreat at your next student program.
- Ask students to share stories in front of the entire group of how they are seeing the Holy Spirit at work in their lives and also in their friends' lives.
- Follow up on new students who came to the retreat and make sure they stay connected in the ministry.
- Follow up immediately on students who made decisions to trust Christ.
- Use the momentum of the retreat and keep building upon it by regularly meeting together.
- Continue teaching topics related to the retreat theme of the power of the Holy Spirit.
- Challenge students to keep praying for their friends. Keep verbalizing the value of evangelism and praying together as a ministry.
- Encourage leaders to continue building relationship with the students in their small groups and to check on areas in which students committed to grow.
- Provide opportunities for students to maintain the bonds they built by implementing or continuing a small group ministry and placing students on campus teams.
- Evaluate the retreat by asking the following questions:
  Did the facility serve us well? Would we go there again?
  Did we promote the retreat far enough in advance?
  How did students respond to the speaker?
  Would we ask him or her to speak at next year's camp?
  Did the programming elements flow together smoothly?
  How did we do financially?
  Do we need to budget more money next year?
  Was the schedule too packed or was there the right amount of free time?
  Did we have the right leaders and enough volunteers to help?
  What did we learn?
  How can next year's retreat be better?
- Write thank-you notes to your leaders, speaker, and musicians.
- Call or write the campsite and thank the personnel for their help in making your retreat run smoothly.
- Take time to celebrate with your staff and/or leadership team the amazing things God did at the retreat.
- Rest!

Student Notes # 1
Saturday Morning Quiet Time

If you are reading this, then you have made the choice to start your day with the One who created you and wants to have a relationship with you. God is delighted that you want to learn how to talk to Him. Take out your Bible and enjoy the next 20–30 minutes learning more about Him.

The following verses are found in the book of Psalms, which were mostly written by David. He spoke very intentionally to God from his heart. God really wants to hear from you . . . from *your* heart. Let's see what David said to his Maker.

Psalm 86

Hear, O Lord, and answer me, for I am poor and needy.
Guard my life, for I am devoted to you.
You are my God; save your servant who trusts in you.
Have mercy on me, O Lord, for I call to you all day long.
Bring joy to your servant, for to you, O Lord, I lift up my soul.
You are forgiving and good, O Lord, abounding in love to all who call to you.
Hear my prayer, O Lord; listen to my cry for mercy.
In the day of my trouble I will call to you, for you will answer me.
Among the gods there is none like you, O Lord;
no deeds can compare with yours.
All the nations you have made will come and worship before you, O Lord;
they will bring glory to your name.
For you are great and do marvelous deeds; you alone are God.
Teach me your way, O Lord, and I will walk in your truth;
give me an undivided heart, that I may fear your name.
I will praise you, O Lord my God, with all my heart;
I will glorify your name forever.
For great is your love toward me;
you have delivered me from the depths of the grave.
The arrogant are attacking me, O God;
a band of ruthless men seeks my life–men without regard for you.
But you, O Lord, are a compassionate and gracious God,
slow to anger, abounding in love and faithfulness.
Turn to me and have mercy on me; grant your strength to your servant
and save the son of your maidservant.
Give me a sign of your goodness, that my enemies may see it and be put to shame, for
you, O Lord, have helped me and comforted me.

Take a few minutes to reread this psalm and then work through the following:

- Can you find David praising God in this prayer?
- Is David requesting something from God? How does he ask?
- Circle any parts of this prayer that challenge your prayer life.
- Write a simple prayer of your own to God. Speak to Him from your heart. He is listening intently.

Student Notes #2
Letter from God

Dear Child of Mine,

You are officially invited by Me to a meal in your honor. You will be seated at the King's table and served by the King Himself. Please, come as you are . . . don't change on account of My presence. Just bring an open heart and pure motives. And when the bread is broken–I'll break it for you. The wine, when it is poured–I'll pour it for you. And when your burdens are lifted, it's because I have drawn near to take them from you.

Sometimes others think that they need to perform at these dinners, but not you, not tonight. I want you to leave the chores of life and enter into My splendor. Relax. Let Me serve you.

This is the way I meant it to be from the beginning.

I love you, My child.

Come.

Lovingly,

Jesus

P.S. I will meet you at the table–watch for Me! I'll be wearing the apron.

Student Notes #3
Sunday Morning Quiet Time

We are so glad that you have decided to take some personal time to worship your God and Savior. This morning, we have listed for you a number of different names that are used for God. Take the next 15–20 minutes to read them three times. First, read through them slowly. Then read them aloud slowly. Finally, circle the names that have been true in your life recently. When you have finished each of the three reading exercises, take five minutes to pray and thank God for the ways that He has revealed Himself to you in the past. Then ask God to show Himself to you in ways that you have not yet experienced.

Names, Titles, and Descriptions of God

God of Forgiveness	God of Refuge	God of Strength
God of Peace	Father of Compassion	Father to the Fatherless
God Almighty	God My Rock	Stronghold
God of Glory	God of Grace	God of Hope
God of Love	God of Truth	God Our Strength
Spirit of Faith	God of Encouragement	Lord
God the Potter	My Hope	My Strong Deliverer
God Who Gives Endurance	My Advocate	My Helper
God of Wisdom	The God of Provision	My Hiding Place
My Light	Holy One	My Friend
Jesus	Alpha and Omega	Bread of Life
Great Shepherd	My Intercessor	God of Salvation
Teacher	God of Second Chances	Holy Spirit
God of Servanthood	God of Miracles	God of Healing
My Song	My Support	God Who Hears Prayer
Our Judge	Our Leader	God of Promises
God Who Judges Righteously	Lord Who Is There	Lord Our Shield
Sanctuary	Refiner and Purifier	Wonderful Counselor
The Life	Spring of Living Water	

I AM

Share one of your underlined names with a friend today.

Appendix A
Leader Responsibility Sheets

Responsibilities of D-Team Leaders

Thank you for your willingness to use your gifts as you serve at camp. Your contribution is valued and needed! Realize that you are helping to lead the charge at camp, and we are counting on your wisdom, maturity, and commitment. While at camp, if you have any questions or situations that require assistance or counsel, please see the ministry or camp director.

We've listed a few suggestions for you to think through and ways that you can demonstrate leadership as you prepare for your role at the upcoming camp. Take some time to read through the list and ask God to give you discernment, wisdom, and strength as you lead.

Benchmarks

This camp/retreat is a perfect opportunity for you to initiate needed steps of spiritual growth in the lives of your D-Team small group members. This might be the time to challenge your students on that issue you've been praying about. For example, you might say, **"Maybe some of you need to get serious about your quiet times with the Lord. Are you shortchanging God and yourself? Make this the day that you start on a path of consistent quiet times."** Spend some time with the Lord to discern the challenge He may have for your students. Ask yourself, *What action is the Lord guiding me to create in the lives of the students He has put under my charge?* This camp/retreat could create these kinds of "benchmark moments."

Busing

Use the time on the road to and from the retreat or camp to set the right tone for the weekend. You can do this through your conversations and in the way you act (and drive). "Hang out" purposefully. Ask questions like **"What do you want to get out of this camp or retreat? How are you doing these days spiritually?"** Your time in the car or bus on the way home is especially important. Ask students individually what God taught them and in what ways they grew. You are also responsible for making sure that students do not get too rowdy or too loud. Be sure to help with the loading of the bus after meal stops in order to keep us on schedule. Students are not allowed to change buses at meals or other nonscheduled stops. Be prepared to help on the way home as well.

Cabin Check-in/Checkout

If you have housing problems during cabin check-in, please record all problems on paper and come to the camp office. Housing problems will be handled by the ministry or camp director. You are responsible for the cleanliness of your cabin at checkout. Please make sure students respect the camp and its property. Leave the cabins cleaner than when you arrived.

Cabin Check and Lights Out

You are responsible to have your students in their cabins before cabin check and to have the cabin quiet with lights out at curfew. Someone will come to your cabin each night to take attendance. Please do not be late for cabin checks. It is important that each student is accounted for and that no one is missing.

Find a Place

As soon as you get to the camp/retreat, begin to think about the best place for your D-Team to meet. Designate a meeting place so that everyone knows where you will meet for D-Teams after the messages. Pick a place that is free from distractions and that is conducive to meaningful discussions.

Injuries and Medications

If you or a student is injured during camp, report the injury to the nurse immediately. Do not attempt to move the injured person or take the injured person to the nurse. All students' medications, prescription and nonprescription, must be given to the nurse at registration.

Leadership Meetings
We will hold at least one leadership meeting each day to discuss the day's schedule, pray together, and give you an opportunity to share stories of how you see God working. Feel free to raise any concerns or questions you may have at these meetings. Please check the schedule for the exact times and location.

Lost and Found
Lost and found is located at the camp main desk. Please retrieve lost items and turn in found items there.

Notes
A card or note from you to the students God has put under your charge means a lot to them. There are some things that are best said on paper, like: "I believe in you"; "I'm proud of you"; or "I see a lot in you–Let me tell you what I see." Let God use you to encourage and inspire students. For those of you who are beginning new D-Teams at this camp/retreat, you may want to write some introductory letters telling your students that you are looking forward to all that God is going to do in their lives. Write these notes prior to the camp or retreat and give each student his or her note sometime during the camp experience. These kind of notes really do touch the hearts of students.

Personal Time
During most of this camp/retreat, you will be surrounded by people. For some leaders, this poses no problem. For others, it is very draining. Your time alone will be limited, so prepare yourself in advance as much as possible. If you need time alone to stay fresh and focused, perhaps waking up 30 minutes early and going for a walk would help.

Programs and Messages
Please make sure you and your students bring Bibles, notebooks, and pens to every session. You may not have time to go back to your cabin before the morning message so come to breakfast prepared. During the sessions, sit with the students in your small group and encourage them to be attentive.

Discourage students from talking during the messages and remind them to take notes whenever possible.

Stick Together
Tell your "teammates" that this weekend you need to stick together. Make sure that this is one of the first things that they hear from you. Communicate to them that it's important to eat together, sit together in the sessions, and hang out together recreationally (with other D-Teams if you choose). Being together will create bonds and memories.

Student Ownership
You are not expected to be a baby-sitter or a police officer. Your role is to be a shepherd and leader. If your students are not willing to follow your lead, talk to the camp director.

Student Participation
Make sure your students attend all meals and sessions and participate in competition. Please do not allow students to sleep in and miss breakfast or the morning session. If your student is sick or injured, he or she must report to the camp nurse.

Trash and Camp Condition
Your leadership from Day One of camp is imperative. Please do not allow students to abuse the camp with trash or misconduct. Vandalism will result in a student's expulsion at his or her parents' expense.

Walks
Long walks, one-on-one, are a great way to build relationships with each of your students. Your goal should be to take a walk with each one of your students. Let your students get to know you even better. Be transparent. Ask pointed questions. Pray together.

Appendix B
One-on-One Questions

Here are some suggested questions your students can use for One-on-Ones during camp. Choose one or two questions each day for students to ask their one-on-one partner. Or copy the list and place it on tables before lunch or dinner so students can select their own questions. These questions will help facilitate discussion and give students an opportunity to get to know others better. Feel free to come up with your own questions to add to the list.

1. If you could move anywhere in the world, where would you live, and why?
2. Who was/is your favorite teacher?
3. If you could ask God any question face-to-face, what would it be?
4. What is your favorite Bible verse or story?
5. Who is your favorite biblical character and why?
6. What do you like best about high school? What do you like least?
7. What do you like best about our student ministry?
8. If your house was on fire and you only had enough time to save three material possessions, what would you choose? (All your family members are safe.)
9. What four words would you use to describe your mom? Your dad?
10. If you could have lunch with anyone, who would you choose?
11. How many brothers/sisters do you have? How do you get along?
12. What is one of your pet peeves?
13. Right now, what would your dream job look like?
14. What do you think you will do after high school?
15. If you were stuck on a deserted island for one year with two other people, who would you want those two people to be?
16. What is one of your favorite childhood memories?
17. What do you like to do in your free time?
18. What would you do if you were given one million dollars?
19. What do you think is the best thing about being a teenager? What is the worst thing?
20. If you could not fail, what would you try tomorrow?
21. Whom do you respect and why? Do you have a role model?
22. If you could do one miracle, what would you do?
23. What are two things for which you are grateful to God?
24. What is your most embarrassing moment? Can you share it with me?
25. In what area of your Christian life do you desire to grow? How do you plan to make it happen?

Appendix C
Suggested Worship Chorus List

"As the Deer" by Maranatha Singers (*Praise 8*, Maranatha! Music, 1984)

"As We Seek Your Face" by Maranatha Singers (*Praise 14*, Dave Bilbrough Songs and Thankful Music, 1990)

"Awesome God" by Rich Mullins (*Jesus Mighty God/ The Praise Band*, Edward Grant Inc., 1988)

"Awesome in This Place" by Integrity Hosanna! (*The Secret Place*, Integrity's Hosanna! Music, 1992)

"The Beauty of Holiness" by Steve Camp and Rob Frazier (*Mercy in the Wilderness*, Word Music, 1994)

"Cry of My Heart" by Terry Butler (*Praise Band 4*, Maranatha, Mercy Publishing, 1992)

"Don't Forget His Benefits" by Tommy Walker (*Live Worship with Tommy Walker & the C.A. Worship Band*, Doulos Publishing and WeMobile Music, 1994)

"Great Are Your Works" by Andy Park (*Draw Me Closer, Songs of the Vineyard*, Mercy Publishing, 1987)

"Heaven Is in My Heart" by Graham Kendrick (*Public Praise Integrity Hosanna! Music: Crown Him*, Make Way Music, 1991)

"I Love Your Grace" by Rick Founds (*Praise Band 3 Everlasting*, Maranatha! Music, 1990)

"I Will Never Be" by Geoff Bullock (*Shout to the Lord*, Integrity Music, 1996)

"Jesus, Lover of My Soul" by John Ezzy, Daniel Grul, and Stephen McPherson (*Shout to the Lord*, Integrity Music, 1996)

"Let the Redeemed" by John Barnett (*Give Thanks–Praise & Worship*, Vineyard Ministries International, 1989)

"Let the Walls Fall Down" by John Barbour, Anne Barbour, and Bill Batstone (*Raise the Standard*, Maranatha! Music, 1993)

"Lord, I Lift Your Name on High" by Rick Founds (*Praise Band 1: Jesus, Mighty God*, Maranatha! Music, 1989)

"Pour Out My Heart" by Craig Musseau (*Light the Fire Again: Touching the Father's Heart Vineyard #18*, Vineyard/Mercy Publishing, 1994)

"Power of Your Love" by Geoff Bullock (*Shout to the Lord*, Integrity Music, 1996)

"A Pure Heart" by Rusty Nelson (*Take the City*, Integrity Hosanna! Music, 1992)

"Shine, Jesus, Shine" by Graham Kendrick (*Amazing Love*, Make Way Music/Integrity Hosanna!, 1987)

"Shout to the Lord" by Darlene Zschech (*Shout to the Lord*, Integrity Music, 1996)

"Show Me Your Ways" by Russell Fragar (*Shout to the Lord*, Integrity Music, 1996)

"Sure Foundation" by Don Harris (*The Highest Place*, Integrity Hosanna! Music, 1991)

"Sweet Presence of Jesus" by Tommy Walker (*Live Worship with Tommy Walker and the C.A. Worship Band*, Doulos Publishing & WeMobile Music, 1994)

"We Believe in God" by Amy Grant and Wes King (*Songs From the Loft*, Reunion Records, 1993)

"With Our Heart" by Don Harris (*Pure Heart*, Integrity Hosanna!, 1991)

Music Resource: interl'inc (a music resource organization) Call 1.800.725.3300 for more information.

Retreat Timeline

Task	Completion date

Define the Purpose
Identify the needs of your target
Choose your content
Choose your theme

Prepare in Advance
Check dates
Start your retreat notebook
Choose the facility and negotiate contract
Contract your speaker
Arrange transportation
Determine meeting space setups
Choose your meals
Organize registration
Recruit volunteers
Meet with volunteer leaders
Finalize housing
Confirm all
Develop a contingency plan

Program for Success
Organize your retreat schedule
Plan your sessions: Cue Sheets
Develop or find your curriculum for small groups
Rent needed equipment
Develop competition
Select a speaker

Promote the Event
Develop your marketing strategy
Event brochure
Parent consent form
Event information sheets
Develop announcement schedule
Create video clips or posters
Use testimonies from students whose lives were changed at camp
Leader memos and meeting invites

Pray
Plan prayer times at staff meetings
Recruit a parent volunteer team to pray
Ask church elders to pray

Appendix E
Retreat Budget

Formula: All expenses divided by the *least* number of participating students equals the break-even point.

example:	Expenses	Students	Break-Even	Round-Up
	5405	40	113	125

Additional income
- If 45 students attend 625
- If staff pays $50 each 500
- plus 1125

Sample Budget	Per Person	Group (X 55)
45 students, 10 adults (approx. 1 to 5 ratio)		

	Per Person	Group (X 55)
Room & Board	50	2750
Transportation	10	550
Programming cost		825
Printing		150
Postage		50
Speaker		150
Rented equipment		300
VIP gifts		30
Student "goodies"		150
Competition		150
Miscellaneous		150
Administrative		150
Total		**5405**

Appendix F
Seating Layout

Auditorium Seating

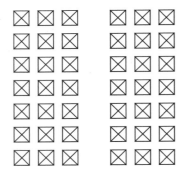

All chairs facing the front of the room

Classroom Seating

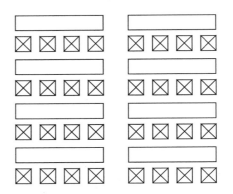

4 chairs on one side of the table
(usually 8'x18")
facing the front of the room

Seminar Seating

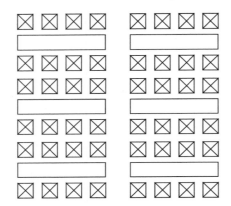

4 chairs on each side of the table
(usually 8'x30")

Hollow Square Seating

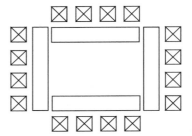

Chairs on the outside of square
with 4 chairs on each side

Circle Seating

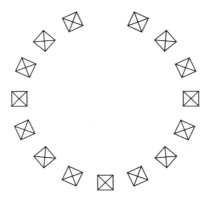

Chairs in a circle

Appendix G
Speaker Contract

Thank you for being an important part of our retreat/camp. We look forward to our time together. Please take a moment to complete this form. It will help us to serve you more effectively. If you need any additional information, please do not hesitate to contact us.

Name: _____

Mailing Address: _____

City: _____ Zip: _____

Phone: _____ Fax: _____

There is audio equipment available for your use. However, it does need to be reserved. Please write what kind of equipment you would like for each session. Equipment includes video, overhead, slide projector, dry marker board, or easel with paper. If you have a special request, please write it in and we will let you know if it is available.

Honorarium
We would like to offer you an honorarium of $ _____ . To ease any distribution confusion, we will mail your honorarium to you one week after camp. If you are unable to fulfill your commitment, your honorarium will be forfeited.

Room and Board
Room and food will be provided during your time at the camp/retreat. You will be provided with a double room.

Room Dates Included: _____

Meals Included: _____

Travel
We will cover any travel expenses up to $_____.

Alternative Dispute
In the unlikely event a claim or controversy should arise, the parties agree to first seek resolution by the biblical means of conciliation and further agree to submit such dispute, claim, or controversy to the Association of Christian Conciliation Services.

Moral Conduct
Please understand that you were carefully chosen to address the topic that is stated in this agreement. Our ministry endeavors to hold the highest moral and ethical conduct for all its leaders. Therefore, we reserve the right to terminate your speaking involvement with the camp/retreat if there is a case for moral or spiritual impropriety.

Signed:_____ Date:_____
Ministry Representative

Signed:_____ Date:_____
Camp/Retreat Speaker

Appendix H
Registration Floor Plan

Girls Luggage area

Solutions table

Guys Luggage area

Nurse: Register Medications

Registration A-M

Registration N-Z

Appendix I
Consent Form

General Release and Hold Harmless Agreement

The undersigned or a member of the immediate family of the undersigned desires to participate in various programs, events, or activities (hereinafter collectively referred to as
"Activities") operated or sponsored by the _____ Church (hereinafter
referred to as "Church"), _____ Youth Ministry (hereinafter referred to
as "Youth Ministry"), and _____ Camp (hereinafter referred to as "Camp").

The undersigned or a member of the immediate family of the undersigned further understands and acknowledges that the undersigned or a member of the immediate family of the
undersigned may incur personal injury or bodily damage while participating in such
Activities.

The undersigned or a member of the immediate family of the undersigned further understands and acknowledges that the Church, Youth Ministry, and the Camp would not allow the
undersigned or a member of the immediate family of the undersigned to participate in such
Activities without releasing and holding harmless the Church, Youth Ministry, and the Camp.

Further, the undersigned or a member of the immediate family of the undersigned request
that the Church, Youth Ministry, and the Camp in consideration thereof agree to hereby
release, and forever discharge the Church, Youth Ministry, and the Camp, their officers and
directors, and their employees, and their agents, and any parties volunteering on behalf of the
Church, Youth Ministry, and the Camp from all actions, claims, costs, expenses or damages of
any kind growing out of or related to any Activity of the Church, Youth Ministry, or the Camp in
which undersigned or a member of the immediate family of the undersigned participates.

The undersigned or a member of the immediate family of the undersigned further acknowledges that this is a full and complete release for all injuries and damages which the undersigned or a member of the immediate family of the undersigned may sustain as a result of the
undersigned or a member of the immediate family of the undersigned participation in any
Church program.

I, _____ , being the legal guardian of
_____ give my permission for him/her to go to
_____ at the _____ Camp under the direction of Youth Ministry. The
undersigned, being a parent and/or guardian of the above minor, does hereby authorize the
treatment of the above minor by a qualified and licensed medical doctor in the event of a
medical emergency which, in the opinion of the attending physician, may endanger his/her
life, cause disfigurement, physical impairment, or undue discomfort if delayed, while said
minor is participating in the above event, including transportation to and from the event site.
This authority is granted only after a reasonable attempt has been made to contact me.

Medical Information
Please list any allergies, medications, medical information, or chronic illnesses your student
may have on the back of this form.

Signed:_____ Dated: _____
(participant's parent/legal guardian)

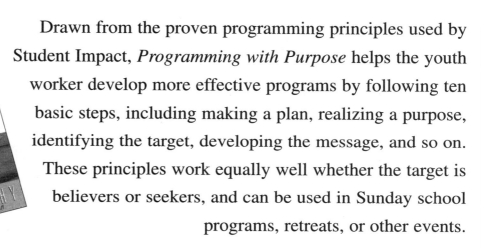

MORE GREAT RESOURCES FOR STUDENT MINISTRY FROM STUDENT IMPACT

Small Group Resources
Bo Boshers
and the Student Impact Team

Small groups create tremendous opportunities for growth, and Small Group Resources will help your youth ministry do that. Each of the books in the Student Impact Small Group Resources series provide a complete short-course curriculum for a quarter's worth of small group meetings.

Volume 1: *Walking with Christ: Twelve Lessons That Will Change Your Life*
Softcover: 0-310-20124-1

Volume 2: *Compassion for Lost People: Twelve Lessons That Will Change Your Friends' Lives*
Softcover: 0-310-20126-8

Volume 3: *Learning to Serve: Twelve Lessons That Will Build the Church*
Softcover: 0-310-20127-6

Volume 4: *A Lifelong Calling: Twelve Lessons That Will Impact the World*
Softcover: 0-310-20128-4

Impact Sports
Bo Boshers and Troy Murphy

Presenting *Impact Sports*—competitive activities with a clear-cut ministry purpose. They're fun, and they're great for building relational bridges for energetic seekers in a natural and exciting way.
Softcover: 0-310-20130-6

Look for Student Impact Small Group Resources & *Impact Sports* at your local Christian bookstore.

ZondervanPublishingHouse
Grand Rapids, Michigan 49530
http://www.zondervan.com